j639.22 Cook, Joseph J. cop 7
COO
Coastal fishing
for beginners

Coastal Fishing
for Beginners

COASTAL FISHING

Joseph J. Cook and

*Books by Joseph J. Cook
and William L. Wisner*

Coastal Fishing for Beginners
Blue Whale, Vanishing Leviathan
The Nightmare World of the Shark
The Phantom World of the Octopus and Squid
Killer Whale!

FOR BEGINNERS

William L. Wisner

Illustrated by Jan Cook

DODD, MEAD & COMPANY
New York

cop 7

1 2 3 4 5 6 7 8 9 10

Library of Congress Cataloging in Publication Data

Cook, Joseph J
    Coastal fishing for beginners.

    Includes index.
    SUMMARY: Discusses tackle, fishing techniques, and
the bait used for saltwater fishing and describes the
various fish commonly found in coastal waters.
    1. Saltwater fishing—United States—Juvenile litera-
ture. 2. Marine fishes—United States—Juvenile litera-
ture. [1. Saltwater fishing. 2. Fishes. 3. Fishing]
I. Wisner, William L., joint author. II. Cook, Jan.
III. Title.
SH457.C79   639'.22   77-6488
ISBN 0-396-07487-1

To Tom Fote and the late James Smith

Contents

Foreword

Coastal fishing, in the waters hugging the shoreline of the United States, offers untold enjoyment to countless millions of male and female anglers of all ages. This enjoyment is as varied as the anglers who seek the many species of fish inhabiting the shallows and depths of these waters.

Because this book is aimed at the angler new to the sport, it will concentrate on species for which beginners are likely to fish, accenting the more popular kinds and those caught from shore, piers, and small boats in sheltered waters. It will consider the less complicated rigs and methods, along with tackle that is relatively simple, inexpensive, easy to wield, and of widest possible service.

For many anglers there is a mystery in fishing—the mystery of staring at the water's surface while wondering what creatures are hidden in the shadows of the sea. For others fishing is suspense—the suspense of never being sure what species or size of fish may be caught. Still other anglers enjoy matching their wits and skills against wild, wily fishes. Feeling the fish strike the bait, setting the hook in its jaw, and the action that follows are the heights of excitement.

Most anglers share all of these emotions, and more—the "more" being a special feeling for the sun, sea, clouds, tides, winds, and rain, a feeling that makes coastal fishing a sport standing alone and above all other sports.

Coastal Fishing
for Beginners

 1

Becoming a Good Angler

To become a good angler you must understand some basic fishing precepts. The better you understand them, the more fish you will catch. And it follows that the more fish you catch, the more enjoyment you will have from your chosen sport.

The following suggestions should help you become a better angler:

1. Learn all about the fishes you seek—their habits and movements—the places they frequent—where and at what depths they feed—the months they are most likely to be in your area—and, perhaps most important, what they eat.

2. Become familiar with the places you fish. Wise anglers learn such details as water depths—nature of the bottom (sandy, muddy, rocky, and so forth)—location of currents (many times currents are particularly important because

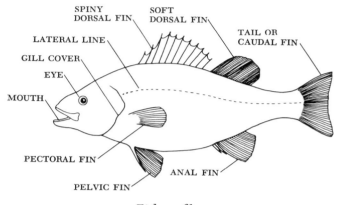

Fish profile

they carry the food that attracts sport fishes)—the rocky
areas, holes, reefs, and wrecks that may harbor fishes.

3. If you decide to become a surf or shore angler, scout a
beach before you begin fishing. Look for likely spots such as
inlets, holes, channels, "white water" caused by currents, and
sloughs (deep water) alongside sandbars off the beach. To
detect deeper places, climb the highest sand dune or some
other natural object—the deeper areas are easy to find because the water there appears darker than that around them.
Polaroid sunglasses will help you see the deeper water by
screening out glare.

4. Watch for helpful hints from nature. Gulls and other
seabirds hovering low over an area and swooping downward
may indicate a school of sport fish at the surface. Also, look
for surface disturbances caused by such schools. They can
make the water "boil" and sometimes you can see their prey
leaping into the air in efforts to escape them.

5. Read all that is available on the subject. Don't hesitate to add to your knowledge of fishing by asking questions of other anglers and all who are interested in fishing. Listen carefully to tackle-shop proprietors, boat captains and mates, fishing station and pier operators, as well as other anglers. Watch experienced anglers in action.

6. Never hesitate to experiment. Try out ideas of your own. That is the way all sport fishing began and that is the way it will be improved.

7. When you learn a new angling procedure, find out "why" its steps are performed, not just how. Once you understand the why, the procedures become routine—like riding a bicycle.

8. Always be a true sportsman. In angling, true sportsmen never keep more fish than they can use at home or give to relatives, friends, and neighbors. You may continue fishing after you have caught your quota, but release surplus fish by unhooking them carefully, handling them as little as possible, and returning them unharmed to the water. If you work quickly, it is possible to get a picture of your catch before you release it. A true sportsman never keeps an undersized fish but releases it to live and grow larger. Also, true sportsmen are considerate of the rights of others. They do not litter, dump garbage into the water, or damage property. Conservation must be every angler's objective; otherwise there will be no fishing in the years to come.

9. Above all, fish. Reading books and articles about coastal fishing will help tremendously, but there is no substitute for actual fishing. Never be afraid of making mistakes. Everyone makes them, even experts. The important thing is to learn from your mistakes.

10. Remember—safety first! Fishing is probably the safest sport there is. But fishing demands good judgment.

Before heading out to the open water in a boat, ALWAYS obtain an official weather report and have:
—an approved Coast Guard life belt or preserver for each person
—oars, anchor, and strong rope
—a reliable compass and a working flashlight
—a large container of fresh water
—fuel, tools, spare parts for the motor, if you are using one.
NEVER stand up in a small boat that is being bounced around by choppy waters. Before going out in a boat it is wise to leave word on shore, at home or at the dock about where you expect to go and approximately when you think you will be back. This could save precious time should it become necessary to look for you.

When shorefishing, ALWAYS exercise caution when:
—climbing around rock jetties, which often have slippery rocks
—wading in unfamilar areas where there may be unseen holes
—going out to a sandbar that is exposed at low tide but becomes covered with water when the tide rises.
NEVER wade out to cast in places where there may be a treacherous undertow.

ALWAYS carry a first-aid kit with you, whether fishing from shore or boat. Safety adds enjoyment to any sport.

~~~~~~~~~~~~~~~~~~~~~~ 2

Tackle

Fishing tackle includes rods, reels, lines, leaders, hooks, and lures. (Lures are also called artificials.) These items are the tools of an angler.

For simplicity, coastal fishing tackle may be divided into two basic types: conventional and spinning. There is another type of tackle, for fly-fishing, but this is an advanced, specialized technique best used by highly experienced anglers.

Years ago most fishing rods were made from wood, though some were of metals such as steel and copper. Today practically all rods are made of fiber glass, a strong, rugged, very durable material that cannot rot, rust, or corrode because it is unaffected by water. Fiber-glass fishing rods give years of service, without the maintenance required by wooden and metal models. There are good ones that everyone can afford.

The most obvious difference between conventional and spinning tackle is in the reels. A reel is a device having a spool set in a frame which is mounted on the handle or butt

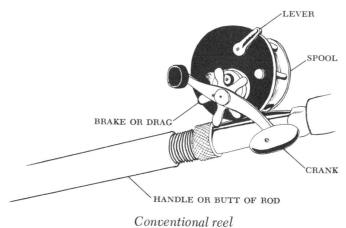

Conventional reel

of a fishing rod. The spool stores the line. The purpose of the reel is to control the movement of the fishing line.

On a conventional reel, the spool revolves. The spool on a spinning reel does not turn but remains stationary. It is easy to demonstrate the difference in their operation.

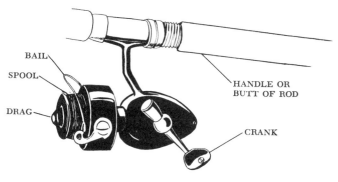

Spinning reel

Obtain a spool of ordinary sewing thread to represent the fishing reel. To imitate a conventional reel, hold the spool lightly between thumb and forefinger, its long axis parallel to your body, the loose end of its thread pointing away from you. With your free hand, pull out the loose end of the thread. As the thread goes out, the spool turns. Fishing line on a conventional reel operates the same way. To get the fishing line back on the spool, you must turn the reel's crank, whereupon the spool revolves in the opposite direction, taking in the line.

To imitate a spinning reel, hold the spool of thread at one end, its long axis pointing away from you. With your free hand, slowly pull the thread directly away from you. Notice how the thread leaves the spool in coils since the spool cannot turn. Line leaves a spinning reel in the same manner. To retrieve the line, spinning reels have a mechanism, called a bail, that gathers in the line as you turn the crank, depositing it back on the spool.

Conventional and spinning reels are mounted differently and the rods are different. Spinning reels are mounted underneath the rod while conventional reels are mounted on top of the rod. Conventional rods have guides, usually made of metal loops, spaced along the top of the rod to allow the fishing line to run in a straight course from the reel to the tip of the rod. Spinning rods have the guides on the bottom side of the pole. Since the line leaves a spinning rod in coils instead of a straight line, the spinning rod has larger guides to handle the coils better. Another difference is that some spinning rods are a bit longer and more flexible than similar conventional models.

Spinning tackle is designed primarily for casting and therefore beginners can learn to cast greater distances more easily with it. Since the reel's spool does not revolve, there

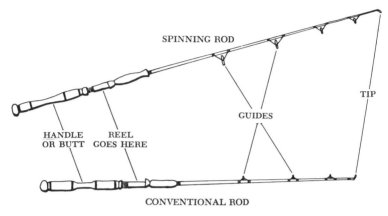

Comparison of spinning and conventional rods

is none of the backlash—fierce line tangle—that can occur when casting with conventional tackle. However, conventional tackle can be superior to spinning equipment in other kinds of angling, such as trolling heavy rigs or fishing the bottom in deep water. The choice of either type of tackle depends greatly upon the method used and the size of the fishes hunted.

All properly designed conventional and spinning reels, even inexpensive models, have a brake or drag. This is a mechanism within the reel that provides resistance when the line is being pulled from the spool. You can vary the amount of resistance, increasing or decreasing it, by adjustment. On conventional reels you tighten or loosen the drag by turning a star-shaped wheel alongside the crank. On a spinning reel, adjustment is usually by means of a knob in front.

The purpose of drag resistance is to help control a fish. Often this is necessary with the larger or particularly hard-fighting species and those that make long runs and might otherwise strip the reel of line. The brake also is useful in trolling. It prevents line from being pulled from the reel by the boat's motion.

Tackle is graded generally as ultra-light, light, medium, heavy, and extra-heavy or big game. These terms do *not* refer so much to the actual weights of the outfits as to the strength of the line used. Fishing lines come in a wide range of breaking strengths, from as light as one-pound test to as heavy as 130-pound test. Most of the line you'll need to hunt for the fishes presented in this book will be in the light class, 15- to 20-pound test at the most.

Practically all fishing lines today are made from synthetic materials such as nylon and Dacron. There are two major types: braided, in which fine strands are twisted upon each other like a rope's fibers; and monofilament, which consists of a single, strong strand. Both types are good, and anglers develop their own preference, as you will.

Whether fishing with a baited hook or with an artificial, a leader (a short length of material for attaching the end of a fishing line to a lure or hook) usually is rigged between the line and the hook or artificial by means of a two-loop barrel

 *Barrel swivel*

swivel. A two-loop barrel swivel consists of two eyes joined by a barrel-shaped pin. The leader protects the line from water action, the teeth of many fishes, and the rubbing friction of sand and rocks, while the two-loop barrel swivel lessens twisting of the leader. The leader may be of monofilament line, nylon leader material, or fine wire. Monofilament line is usually used as a leader with braided line when fishing rocky areas. This is because it is more resistant to

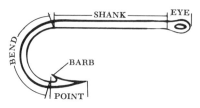

Parts of a fishhook

rubbing by rocks than is braided line. Every angler has his own idea of how long leaders should be. Thus, leader lengths range upward from six inches.

Fishing hooks come in many sizes. No one hook can be effective with all fishes. The choice of an appropriate hook depends upon such elements as size of the fish hunted, type of tackle used, how the fish takes a bait, structure of the fish's mouth, and how hard the fish battles.

There are five parts to a fishing hook; the eye, shank, bend, point, and barb. The eye is where you tie your fishing line or leader; the shank is the long, straight part of the hook; the bend is where the hook turns toward the point; the point is the part of the hook that "hooks" a fish; while the barb "holds" the fish on the point once it is hooked. Good quality hooks are made of steel and have sharp points and strong barbs, and they are treated to resist salt-water rust. Attached to some salt-water fishhooks is a short line called the snell, made of gut or other similar material which attaches the hook to the fishing line or leader.

Unfortunately there is no uniform system of hook classification, as manufacturers determine the various sizes in which their hooks are measured. However, most hooks are divided into two groups.

In the first group, hooks are numbered 1, 2, 3, and so on. No. 10 is the smallest suggested for the fishes in this book.

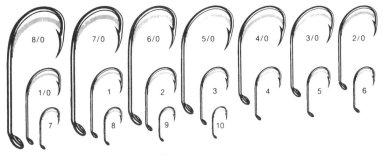

Hook classification

In the second group, hooks are numbered 1/0, 2/0, 3/0, and on up. No. 8/0 is the largest hook suggested for the fishes in this book.

Fishing hooks also come in different designs, the better to catch and hold different kinds of fish. Often these designs are named for the fishermen who created them or the companies that make them. They include such names as Kirby, Mustad, O'Shaughnessy, Eagle Claw, and many others. Variations in design are most noticeable in the length of the shank and in the bend. The Chestertown, for example, has a long

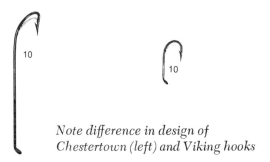

Note difference in design of
Chestertown (left) and Viking hooks

shank. The hook called a Viking has a short one. Many hooks, such as the Sproat and Carlisle designs, have a bend shaped more or less like the letter U. On others the point curves inward more, toward the shank.

Whenever you are in doubt about what size or design hook to use for any fish, ask a tackle-shop operator. He will see that you choose the right one. As you engage in actual fishing, you will learn to choose the right one for yourself.

Remember that hooks should be kept clean and sharp if they are to be effective.

The lure or artificial imitates the natural food of fish and is sometimes used with its own hook attractively baited with natural food. Four of the more commonly used lures are *jigs*, *plugs*, *spoons*, and *metal squids*.

1. *Jigs:* Jigs are made of solid metal, giving them weight. They come in a variety of designs and many of them are shiny, giving them added attraction. Also, many jigs are wrapped with skirts of animal hairs, synthetic fibers, feathers, rubber strips, or metal foil, or a combination of these materials, to increase their attractiveness to fishes.

2. *Plugs:* Plugs are casting lures made from wood, plastic, or glass and are designed to imitate a small baitfish. Plugs come in a variety of shapes, sizes, and colors and are made to travel at different water levels while being reeled in. In this way some plugs are used for surface-feeding fishes, some for deep-dwelling fishes, and some for fishes swimming just below the surface. The design of the plug determines at which water level it will travel while being retrieved.

3. *Spoons:* Spoons are metal lures made in a variety of sizes from an inch up to ten inches in length, most shaped like spoons. Spoons, like plugs, are fished at all water depths, according to their design.

4. *Metal squids:* Squids are shiny, solid metal lures that

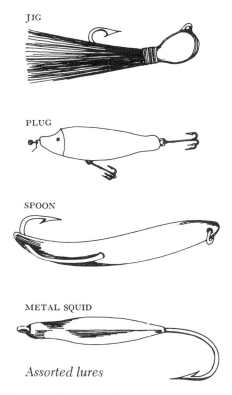

JIG

PLUG

SPOON

METAL SQUID

Assorted lures

come in different shapes and sizes, imitating various small baitfishes. Primarily, metal squids are used when casting, which has become known as squidding.

All lures have the hook or hooks attached to some part of their bodies. Also, all lures have an eye which can be attached either to a fishing line or to a leader.

Sinkers are used only when bottom fishing or when it is necessary to troll deeply. In coastal fishing the two most commonly used sinkers are the bank and pyramid. Both do the job of sending hooks to the bottom and keeping them there. Pyramid sinkers are used over sandy bottoms because

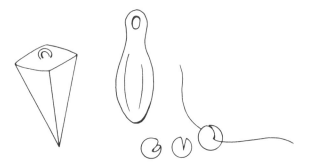

Sinkers—pyramid, bank, and split shot

they dig in and hold, due to their shape. The smoother bank sinkers are used in rocky areas and while drifting because they are less likely to "snag" on rocks and other bottom debris.

Shot sinkers are small and are attached directly to the fishing line or leader. Most shot sinkers have a split running across them. The split in the shot sinker is placed on the line or leader and squeezed tight with your fingers or with a small pliers.

In bottom angling, especially for small fishes, use only enough sinker weight to keep your bait where it belongs. You may have to experiment a little to get the desired weight —just enough to keep your hooks on the bottom but light enough so that you can feel the fighting ability of the hooked fish.

Bobbers or floats are used to keep your hooks off the bottom. The level at which you want your hooks to remain depends upon what species of fish you are seeking and at what level they tend to swim. Bobbers and floats are usually made either of cork or plastic. They are attached directly to your line by means of a clip or snap that is a part of the bobber or float. Choice of what size bobber to use de-

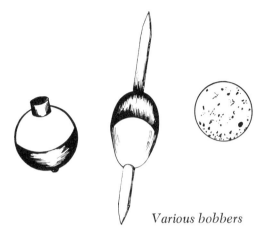

Various bobbers

pends upon size of rig and fish sought, plus weather and water conditions. Large floats or bobbers are used in rough water and when seeking large fish; smaller floats or bobbers are used when seeking smaller fish and when the water is fairly calm.

3

Rigging

There are a number of ways to arrange leaders, hooks, lures, and sinkers so that they do the best job for you, and this arrangement is known as rigging.

When attaching fishing line directly to a snelled hook, lure, leader, or sinker, the Norm Duncan knot is recommended.

To tie a Norm Duncan knot:

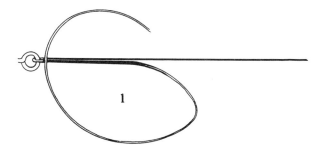

1. Run the end of the fishing line through the eye or loop of a hook, lure, swivel, or leader for at least six inches, and double back.

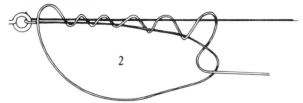

2. Make six turns with the end of the line around the double line and pull the end of the line through the loop.

3. Pull the end of the line until the six turns are snug.

4. Slide the knot against the eye or loop of the hook, lure, swivel, or leader.

When attaching a snelled hook to a leader, slip the looped end of the snelled hook through an eye on the leader or swivel. Then curve the hook back toward the looped end. Now run the hook through the looped end and pull until

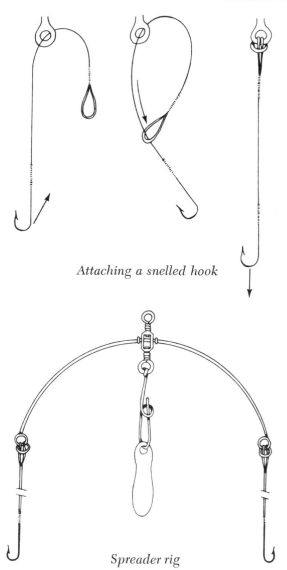

Attaching a snelled hook

Spreader rig

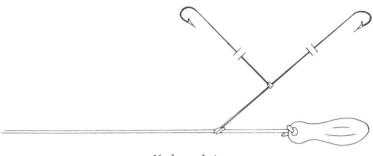

Y-shaped rig

the looped snell is tight against the eye of the leader or swivel.

Five of the more popular rigs are the *spreader, Y-shape, three-way swivel, fish-finder,* and *high-low* rig.

1. A *spreader* is a short length of stiff wire with an eye at both ends. A hook is attached by its snell to each eye. In the middle of the wire is a loop for attachment to the line. Right under the loop is another loop where the sinker is attached. The purpose of a spreader is to prevent the two hooks from tangling.

2. A *Y-shape* rig is made by tying your first hook by its snell, with or without a three-way swivel (so-called because it has three eyes for connectors), to the line just above the sinker. Tie your second hook's snell to the snell of the first hook, at about the middle. This creates a Y-shape rig which not only can be used at anchor or from shore but is sometimes better than a spreader, especially when drifting, because it is less apt to snag on bottom objects.

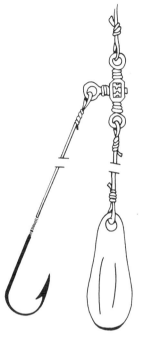

Three-way swivel rig

3. A *three-way swivel* has three eyes attached to a small metal ring. Three-way swivel rigs are created by tying the end of the fishing line to one of the swivel eyes. Then, to one of the two remaining eyes, a sinker heavy enough to keep the rig on the bottom is attached. To the remaining eye is tied about two or three feet of leader (either monofilament or other leader material), and on the leader's end is tied the hook, with or without a snell.

4. A *fish-finder* rig, primarily used when shore casting, calls for a single hook, either a pyramid or round sinker, a leader, a two-way barrel swivel, a swivel snap, and a ring-like connector.

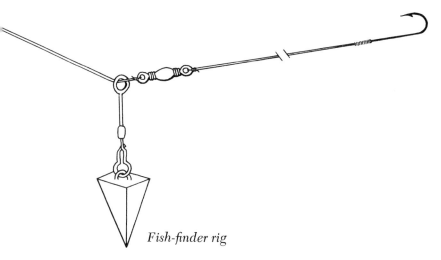

Fish-finder rig

The fish-finder portion of the rig, the ring-like connector, is attached via a swivel snap to the sinker. The end of your fishing line is threaded through the ring-like connector and tied via a two-way barrel swivel to the leader. The single hook is then tied onto the leader. In this rig your sinker will slide freely along the fishing line where it serves two purposes: First—it gives greater maneuverability to the rig while casting, since the force of your cast keeps the sinker as far down on the fishing line as it will go, contributing to the momentum, while carrying the rig out into the water. Second —once cast out and resting on the bottom, the fish-finder keeps your bait close to the sea floor where it belongs, yet the fish-finder is free to slide along the fishing line allowing a fish, when it strikes, to move with the bait unhampered by the sinker.

5. A *high-low* rig uses two hooks. The low hook, on a leader two or three feet long, is attached to the fishing line,

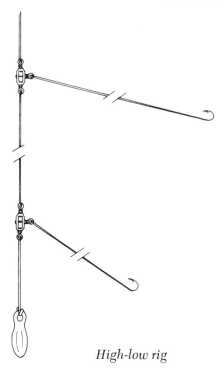

High-low rig

with or without a swivel, one to three feet above the sinker. The high hook, on a leader three to five feet long, is attached in a similar fashion two or three feet above the first hook. This arrangement of hooks covers a fairly wide zone through which fish may be cruising.

4

Feeding Fishes

All angling is based upon one factor—offering fishes something to eat. You may use either bait or a lure or a combination of the two.

Wise anglers always try to find out what natural foods are being eaten that day by the fishes they seek. Whenever possible get that food and use it as bait. If the bait is unobtainable or too expensive, use a lure that imitates it, either by looks or action.

As important as the selection of a bait or lure is the way the bait or lure is presented to the fish. The very best bait or lure cannot be effective if not properly presented.

For example, imagine that the fish you seek feeds on or near the bottom. Any tasty bait or lifelike imitation presented near the surface has little chance of attracting the desired species. Or imagine it the other way around—fishes that normally feed at or near the surface cannot be expected to find offerings that are presented on the bottom.

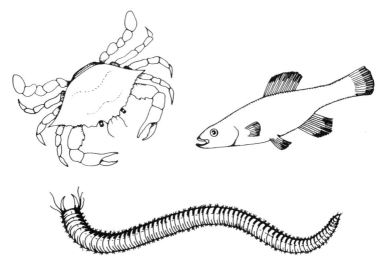

Some natural baits—crab, killy, and marine worm

In order to select and present either baits or lures intelligently you must understand the habits of the fishes you seek. By reading, observing, asking, and actually fishing, you can learn such important basic details about different species of fish as:

1. What they eat: What kinds and types of natural foods do they eat? Do they want their food alive or will they accept it dead? Will they take lures?

2. Where they feed: Do they feed near the surface, on the bottom, or in varying water depths? Do they feed in swift or calm waters? Do they prefer sandy, muddy, or rocky bottoms?

3. How they feed: Do they nibble on a bait or lure or do they immediately take it in their mouths? Do they want a moving or stationary bait?

4. When they feed: Are they day or night feeders? Do tides affect their eating habits?

The proper selection of bait or lure and the proper method of fishing in the most natural way possible are essential to successful coastal fishing.

5

Fishing Methods

Fishing methods are the different techniques of offering fishes something to eat. There are five methods generally employed in coastal fishing, plus one important aid to three of them. The five methods are *bottom fishing, trolling, shore casting, jigging,* and *boat casting.*

1. *Bottom fishing:* This method is commonly known as "sinker bouncing" because at intervals the sinker is bounced on the bay or sea floor to make certain that the rig is all the way down where it should be. Bottom fishing is one of the most popular methods since it can be used for so many species—hundreds of species of salt-water fish may be caught in this way. The method can be used from a boat while at anchor or drifting. At times it is advantageous to allow the boat to drift, thus covering a bigger bottom-fishing area.

2. *Trolling:* This means towing a natural or artificial bait behind the stern of a boat to attract species of fish that

actively pursue prey. Trolling may be done near the surface, near the bottom, or at intermediate levels, depending on the feeding habits of the particular species of fish you seek.

3. *Shore casting:* Originally known as surf casting, this once meant casting into an oceanfront for "battlers" such as bluefish, striped bass, or channel bass feeding just beyond the breakers. Today, the term shore casting means casting from any shore—bay, inlet, sound, or from a jetty, as well as along a surf beach.

Shore casting may be done with either conventional or spinning tackle. Whichever tackle you use, the rod should measure from seven to ten feet in length. The following casting techniques are suggested:

A. Conventional tackle—grasp the rod under the reel with your right hand. Hold the spool of the reel stationary

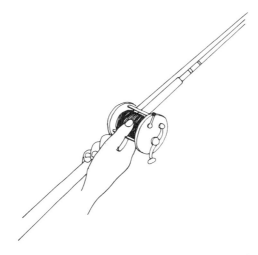

Releasing thumb pressure on a conventional reel

with your thumb. Put the reel into free-spool. (On most conventional reels there is a lever on the upper right side of the reel. Pulling the lever back to you puts the reel into free-spool, allowing you to cast. Pushing the lever forward engages the spool, allowing you to reel in.) Hold the butt of the rod with your left hand, your right hand gripping the rod just behind the reel. Stand sideways with left foot parallel to the water's edge. Hold arms slightly away from your body. You should be in a position somewhat like a batter facing a pitcher. The rod is held in the same position as you would hold a bat. Pivot your shoulders and hips as you swing the rod up and forward. When the rod is almost directly over your head, release enough thumb pressure on the spool to let the line fly out, yet maintain enough pressure to prevent backlash. Keep some thumb pressure on the spool as the bait or lure arches out toward the water. When the bait or lure hits the water, apply strong thumb pressure. This will prevent backlash as your bait or lure settles into the water. Take the reel out of free-spool. You are now ready to bottom fish or retrieve your lure.

All lures are retrieved by cranking the handle of the reel. The speed at which you wish to retrieve the lure depends upon the feeding habits of the fish you seek; some fish like fast-moving prey while others prefer slower-moving prey. Thus, you have to adjust the retrieval of the lure to the feeding preferences of the fish sought.

B. Spinning tackle—face casting area squarely with feet comfortably spaced apart. Pick up line from pickup on spinning reel and rest it across your forefinger, your right hand holding the rod above the reel while your left hand grasps the butt. Swing the rod back and bring it for-

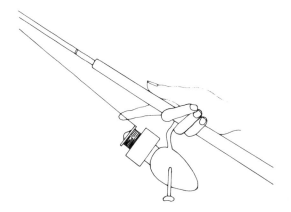

Forefinger pickup of casting line on spinning reel

ward to position directly over your head. While doing this, your left arm pulls down on the butt while your right arm pushes forward on the rod. When the rod is over your head, release the line from your index finger. The line will fly out, and no thumb pressure is needed. Follow through with the rod pointing toward the desired casting area. When bait or lure lands in water, crank the handle one turn. You are now ready to bottom fish or retrieve the lure. If you are left handed, reverse the casting directions.

4. *Jigging:* A bait or lure is lowered to a desired depth; then the angler reels it upward a certain distance, lets it drop back down again, reels it upward, and so on in a continuous process.

One purpose of jigging is to attract fishes that pursue moving bait. Another is to find out at what depths fish are feeding on a certain day. Some species feed at various levels, from the surface to near the bottom, in pursuit of their food. Surface-feeding fishes are often betrayed by agitated water

Gulls often call attention to surface-feeding fishes

and by wheeling, diving gulls feeding on pieces and missed scraps of prey. When there is no evidence of feeding fishes, jigging is an excellent method for finding them.

5. *Boat casting:* This is similar to shore casting, except that the angler is in a boat with the big advantage of being able to reach fishes that are out of casting range from shore. Also, more territory can be covered. Many of the same baits and artificials rigged for shore casting are used in this very exciting and effective method, which is employed when the desired fishes are feeding at or near the surface.

The Aid: Although chumming is not a method, it is an important aid to *bottom fishing, jigging*, and *boat casting*. The purpose of chumming is to attract fishes to your baited hook. Chum can consist of various kinds of fish ground into a mushy pulp, small whole shrimp, pieces of little fishes, minced clams, mussel shells cracked to allow the mollusks' body juices to seep into the sea, or any form of sea life on which fishes feed. Even canned cat food that is made of fish can serve as chum.

The activity consists of dropping or ladling the chum overboard in small quantities at regular intervals. As the chum settles into the water, it attracts to your baited hook fishes which otherwise might pass too far away from you and your rig. It is of the utmost importance to keep the chum going out from your location in an unbroken line, whether it be from shore or from a boat. If the chum line is broken, fishes will swim up to the break in the line, stop, and swim away. They will not continue on toward your baited rig.

Chum also may be placed in a mesh sack and tied to a length of line so it reaches the bottom, where it is bounced on the sea floor. The particles of chum seeping out of the sack attract fishes.

Chum sack (or pot)

Flounders: An Unusual Family

Flounders are members of a large tribe commonly known as flatfishes consisting of more than three hundred species. All have flat, compressed bodies giving them a plate-like appearance.

To add to this unique structure, flounders have both eyes located on one side of the head rather than one eye on each side of the head as other fishes do. Also, the flounder's mouth, situated near the tip of the snout, slants downward toward the rear of the head.

The sighted side of a flounder is pigmented and faces upward. Because of the flattened shape of the flounder, the fins are located along the body's edges.

All species of flatfishes, including flounder, can be identified as either left or right sided. The following helps a fisherman to identify a flounder: with the head pointed away from you, hold the fish between your palms, the fish's lower jaw and your litttle fingers on the bottom. If the flounder's eyes and pigmented side face toward your right hand, the fish is right sided or right eyed. If the eyes and colored side face toward your left hand, the fish is left sided or left eyed.

In fishing for flounder, it is essential that you know which species you are after because tackle, bait, lures, and methods vary.

Winter Flounder

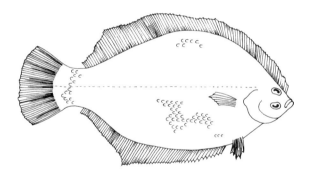

OTHER COMMON NAMES: Spring flounder, fall flounder, black flounder, blackback, flatfish, flatty, flounder, lemon sole, mud dab, and mudback. Larger specimens are called sea flounders, and the largest, because of their shape and size, are known as snowshoes.

SCIENTIFIC NAME: *Pseudopleuronectes americanus*

RANGE: Labrador to Georgia. Some of the greatest centers of abundance are off New England, New York, and New Jersey.

PHYSICAL DESCRIPTION: The winter flounder is right sided and has a small mouth with few teeth and rubbery lips. A straight lateral line extends from its gills to its rounded tail.

The upper side is dark and splotched with shades of black, greenish-brown, reddish-brown, dark slate, or brown mottled with dark gray to black spots.

The underside is predominantly white with a slightly bluish tinge. Occasionally the area near the tail may have a yellowish cast and at times this side may also have dark splotches scattered over its surface.

Winter flounders range in length from six to fifteen inches and in weight from one-half to two pounds, but some open-sea specimens do reach twenty inches and a weight of five pounds.

HABITS: Winter flounders do not like either excessively cold or warm water. They prefer water having a moderate temperature. To satisfy this preference, winter flounders move back and forth between shallow and deep waters, depending upon the seasonal temperature of the sea.

In the spring and fall, shallow waters are more moderate in temperature than deeper water, while in the summer and winter, deeper waters are more moderate than shallow waters. The reason for this is that layers of sea water act as insulators against either frigid air or excessively hot air. Thus, winter flounders are found in shallow waters during the spring and fall, while in the winter and summer they head for deeper waters.

Winter flounder populations are localized, so be careful about over-fishing them. Since there are no migrations from other regions to repopulate an area, when a regional population is depleted that is the end of flounder in that locality.

FISHING PLACES: Winter flounders are bottom fish that prefer a sandy-muddy surface. Water depth ranges from a foot on down to a hundred feet or more. The flounders are distributed widely in bays, channels, and inlet areas depending on seasons.

FISHING SEASONS: Winter flounders can be caught in bays, channels, and inlet areas from late winter (February) to late spring (June) and from early fall (September) to late fall (November).

TACKLE: You can use conventional or spinning tackle. Either way, it should be in the light class—rod five to six feet long, very flexible, with a small reel and light line, about 6-pound test.

HOOKS AND RIGGING: Hooks must be small because of the winter flounder's small mouth. A good hook for winter flounders is the Chestertown design, with its long shank for ease in removing the hook from the fish. Approximate sizes are quite small, No. 10, No. 9, and No. 8.

Usually two hooks are used when fishing for winter flounders. You may attach the hooks either to a spreader or a Y-shape rig. Use a bank sinker with just enough weight, to about five ounces, to keep your rig on the bottom.

BAITS AND LURES: Use only natural bait for winter flounder, no artificials. Best are bloodworms or sandworms, both marine worms. These fish also bite on pieces of clam or mussel.

You can try a bloodworm or sandworm on one hook and clam on another and see which works better. Just as winter-flounder hooks must be small, so too must the piece of bait be. If a hook or bait is too large, a winter flounder will only nibble until the bait is gone, without getting hooked.

FISHING METHODS: Winter flounders always hug the bottom, so keep your hooks there all the time. Always keep your line just taut enough so that you can feel nibbles. Flounders bite gently.

Chumming with cracked mussels often helps. If you are fishing from a boat and lack chum, try stirring up the bottom by dragging the anchor. This dislodges tiny shellfish that attract flounders.

EDIBILITY: Excellent

Summer Flounder

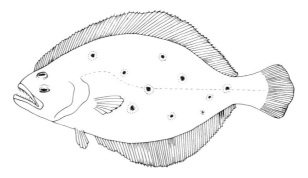

OTHER COMMON NAMES: Fluke and doormat
SCIENTIFIC NAME: *Paralichthys dentatus*
RANGE: Maine to South Carolina, more common from Cape Cod south
PHYSICAL DESCRIPTION: The summer flounder is left sided, with a body that is considerably longer, broader, and heavier than the winter flounder. Another physical difference is the mouth. Unlike a winter flounder, the summer flounder's mouth is large and contains many well-developed, sharp, needle-pointed teeth.

A summer flounder's left or top pigmentation is mainly gray or brown, usually mixed with mottlings of olive, green, orange, or pink, depending on the coloring of the bottom. Usually there are from ten to fourteen darker-colored circular splotches covering this side, while the underside is completely white. Summer flounders are adept at camouflage, and can change the coloring and the circular splotches on the upper side to conform with the bottom. The margin of the tail is rounded when extended.

The summer flounder ranges from two to five pounds, with larger specimens, the doormats, weighing up to fifteen pounds.

HABITS: Summer flounders like warm water. They migrate from ocean waters into protected bays during the warm summer months and re-enter the warmer ocean waters when water temperatures in the bays start to dip in the fall.

Though summer flounders spend most of their lives on or near the bottom, they will scout at intermediate levels when hungry. Being aggressive predators, they will chase small food fishes right to the surface when necessary. They have powerful appetites and devour all kinds of little fishes, shrimp, marine worms, squid, crabs, and other crustaceans, plus various lesser forms of sea life.

FISHING PLACES: Inshore ocean zones and waters in and around inlets, bays, and channels. Summer flounders often frequent inlets and channels because tidal currents bring food their way. Generally they favor a sandy or sandy-mud bottom.

FISHING SEASONS: If bay waters are warm enough, summer flounders start to show in inlets and bays in May, and this best fishing season lasts into the summer. As fall approaches, summer flounders start their return to the ocean.

TACKLE: You can wield either conventional or spinning equipment, and it can be light. The tackle you use for winter flounders also will take summer flounders. If you are fishing in a channel or inlet with strong currents, use 10- or 12-pound test line.

HOOKS AND RIGGING: Since summer flounders have fairly large mouths, use a 1/0 to 5/0 hook, depending upon the weight of the fish currently running. The simplest rig calls for a three-way swivel, just above the sinker, and a hook on a two- or three-foot leader.

BAITS AND LURES: Summer flounders will take any of the following baits: a live killy (marine minnow); silversides (another small fish); a strip of squid or fish; a shrimp; a sandworm; a clam; or a sand eel.

The best bait is a live killy, hooked carefully through the lips so as not to injure it, with a strip of squid dangling and fluttering from the hook. Packages of squid may be bought at most tackle shops.

Some anglers attach spinners ahead of the hook. These are small, shiny metal blades, shaped like the bowl of a teaspoon. As they spin in the water, they shine and flash for added attraction.

Summer flounders also will take small lures trolled near the bottom, but most summer-flounder fishing is done with natural bait.

FISHING METHODS:

1. *Bottom fishing while drifting:* This is the best method. Summer flounder prowl for food and drifting covers a big fishing area. Use a three-way swivel rig with a bank sinker.

2. *Bottom fishing at anchor:* The same rigging and baits used for bottom fishing while drifting are suitable for "still fishing." Cast your line out from the boat, let your rig hit bottom, then reel it slowly along the bottom toward the boat. Repeat until you get a strike. The motion of the bait makes it more attractive. Remember that summer flounder pursue moving prey, and don't forget to chum.

3. *Trolling:* As noted, summer flounders will take small lures trolled near the bottom, so a shiny little spoon or

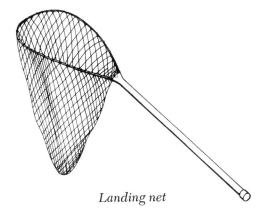

Landing net

feathered jig is generally used. Or try a strip of squid or some of the other natural baits mentioned earlier. You may have to add a small trolling sinker between your fishing line and leader to get your rig down. Trolling will not catch as many summer flounders as bottom fishing, but it is an exciting sport because these fish, being active feeders, strike a moving bait fiercely. There is also the possibility of tying into some other battler, such as a bluefish, striped bass, or weakfish.

4. *Shore casting:* This method is not as productive as bottom fishing but, like trolling, it can bring surprises. It is best done along the channels of inlets where summer flounders cruise in and out in search of food. Rig for the bottom as you would for angling at anchor or drifting. Use the casting procedure suggested for bottom fishing at anchor. Cast to reach the deepest parts of the inlet's channel.

Whatever your method, have a landing net handy. Summer flounder are tricky. They can flip themselves off hooks when being brought out of the water.

EDIBILITY: Excellent

Gulf Flounder

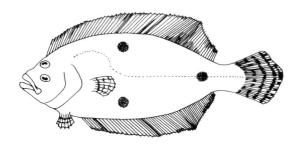

OTHER COMMON NAMES: There may be some local names like "flatty" and "flounder" but these are not widely used.

SCIENTIFIC NAME: *Paralichthys albigutta*

RANGE: North Carolina around Florida to Texas

PHYSICAL DESCRIPTION: Another left-sided flatfish. The top-side color of the Gulf flounder is grayish-brown, marked by a number of pale, rounded splotches that usually run in five lengthwise rows. Three of the more prominent splotches form a triangular design. The under surface is whitish.

Although Gulf flounders can attain a length of fifteen inches, a ten-inch specimen is considered fairly large.

HABITS: The Gulf flounder prefers a sandy bottom over mud and spends most of its time lying on the bottom of bays and close-inshore areas, often partly buried. This species feeds mainly on tiny crustaceans such as shrimp, crabs, and other invertebrates.

FISHING PLACES: Extremely common in the shallower areas of the Gulf of Mexico

FISHING SEASONS: The best fishing occurs from March to October but some Gulf flounder can be hooked all year.

TACKLE: Spinning or conventional, but it must be as light as possible. A light spinning rod provides the most action.

HOOKS AND RIGGING: Hook design is not important but size is. Hooks should be small, like those used for winter flounder, sizes No. 10 to No. 8. Rig for the bottom with a spreader.

BAITS AND LURES: Natural bait, not lures, including shrimp or a piece of clam, crab, or fish in small bits

FISHING METHODS: Bottom fishing at anchor, mainly. Very slow drifting may take some fish.

EDIBILITY: Good, but bones are a nuisance when fish are too small to fillet.

Southern Flounder

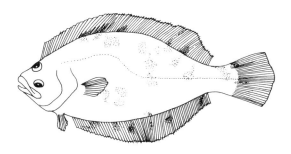

OTHER COMMON NAMES: Southern fluke and mud flounder
SCIENTIFIC NAME: *Paralichthys lethostigmus*
RANGE: North Carolina to Texas

PHYSICAL DESCRIPTION: The left-sided southern flounder, similar in appearance to the summer and Gulf flounders, is distinguished from them by its coloring and markings. The southern flounder's olive-hued dorsal surface blended with indistinct spots is more vivid than the Gulf flounder's duller one. Also, the southern flounder can be distinguished by the absence of the ten to fourteen distinct spots located on the summer flounder's dorsal surface. The belly of the southern flounder is white.

The average size of this species ranges from twelve to twenty inches with weights up to three pounds.

HABITS: Southern flounders prefer brackish water, a mixture of fresh and salt water. They are also caught in full-strength sea water and occasionally in fresh water. No matter what the mixture of water, they prefer shallow depths.

FISHING PLACES: The greatest number of southern flounders are found over muddy bottoms where fresh-water streams flow into bays, lagoons, and sounds.

FISHING SEASONS: All year in the Gulf of Mexico. Summer is best on the Atlantic Coast.

TACKLE: Conventional or spinning, and the lighter the better

HOOKS AND RIGGING: Use small hooks, No. 10 to No. 8. Rig for the bottom with a spreader or a Y-shape rig.

BAITS AND LURES: Most fishing for southern flounders is done with natural baits such as shrimp and small strips of fish. However, this species will also respond to very small spoons bounced slowly along the bottom.

FISHING METHODS: Bottom fishing, at anchor or while drifting

EDIBILITY: Good to excellent

Starry Flounder

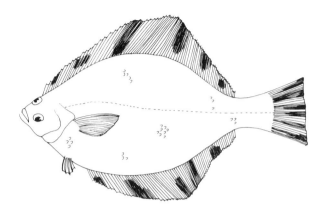

OTHER COMMON NAMES: Great flounder, emery flounder, grindstone flounder, and rough jacket

SCIENTIFIC NAME: *Platichthys stellatus*

RANGE: Alaska southward to central California

PHYSICAL DESCRIPTION: The starry flounder, although it usually has its eyes and pigmentation on the left side, may occasionally be right sided. The mouth is small.

The eyed side is extremely coarse, being covered with sprinklings and splotches of rough black to dark-brown prickly scales. The bottom side is a smooth creamy white. Between the vivid dark bands on the long fins and tail are coloring and tints of orange, yellow, white, and red.

Starry flounder range up to twenty pounds in weight. They rate high as small game fish.

HABITS: The young of this species may be found in brackish water or in completely fresh river water. Young and old starry flounders feed on crustaceans, mollusks, sea worms, and small fishes, including their own relatives.

FISHING PLACES: Close-inshore ocean zones, bays, estuaries, brackish backwaters, and around river mouths

FISHING SEASONS: All year round

TACKLE: In choosing tackle, remember how much these flatfish can weigh. Too, you may be fishing in places where there are brisk currents that require fairly heavy sinkers. To be prepared for such conditions use conventional equipment.

HOOKS AND RIGGING: Hook sizes go from No. 2 for the smaller fish to 1/0 for the heavier ones. Anglers use one or two hooks, with or without leaders, as they prefer. Rig for the bottom as for other flounders.

BAITS AND LURES: Starry flounders have a varied diet that includes shrimp, small crabs, clams, marine worms, and little fishes of different kinds. Therefore, you have a choice of bait. A strip of fish often works best in open water, such as the ocean and large bays, whereas in estuaries and backwater areas such as sloughs and streams the better baits may be sandworm, ghost shrimp, clam, or a piece of crayfish.

FISHING METHODS: With the boat anchored, work your bait in short, halting motions along the bottom.

EDIBILITY: Good

Diamond Turbot

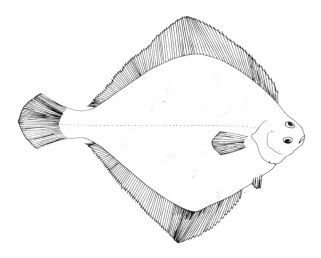

OTHER COMMON NAMES: Diamond flounder, sole, and, incorrectly, halibut

SCIENTIFIC NAME: *Hypsopsetta guttulata*

RANGE: Northern California to the Gulf of California

PHYSICAL DESCRIPTION: The diamond turbot's name is well deserved as its shape resembles a diamond, with the widest part of its body halfway between its mouth and tail. This species has a small mouth and is right sided. The upper side is brown, green, or greenish-brown, peppered with light blue spots which give the fish a mottled appearance. The left or bottom side is white with a distinguishing yellow patch.

Diamond turbots may reach lengths of eighteen inches and weights up to four pounds.

HABITS: Typical of flatfish in general, diamond turbots live and feed on or near the bottom. They may be found over sand or mud in waters ranging from quite shallow to more than 150 feet deep.

FISHING PLACES: These include the inshore ocean belt, surf, bays, and sloughs, often with water less than fifty or sixty feet deep.

FISHING SEASON: All year

TACKLE: Because these are small fish, use light tackle, spinning or conventional. A "bendy" spinning rod is good. Mount a small reel on your rod. Your line should be light, too; 6-pound test is fine.

HOOKS AND RIGGING: Hook size No. 2. Use a Y-shape rig with a bank sinker.

BAITS AND LURES: Use only natural baits—small strips of fish or very small, live fishes; worms, clams, mussels, pieces of crab or crayfish, or ghost shrimp. Inquire locally about what kinds of bait are most effective in the area.

FISHING METHODS: Bottom fishing at anchor, mostly. Some diamond turbot are also caught by bottom fishing in the surf.

EDIBILITY: Very good

7

Marine Basses: Famous Fighters

Marine basses, members of the Serranidae family, have prominent upper lips over large mouths studded with teeth. Their jaws, combined with the solidly built, chunky bodies, make marine basses powerful-looking fish.

Although marine basses have similar basic colorings and markings, individual fish display diversity in vividness of coloration. It is not uncommon for one fish of a species to be intensely pigmented while another fish of the same species is quite dull in its hue. Scientists believe that these differences and changes are caused by the fish's emotions, such as anger and fear.

Except for the striped bass and sea bass, fishes of the Serranidae family do not migrate but prefer to inhabit one specific area. All marine basses favor rocky bottoms where they feed upon smaller fishes and crustaceans.

Striped Bass

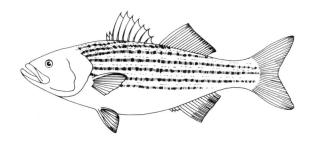

OTHER COMMON NAMES: Striper, rockfish or rock, rock bass, greenhead, white bass, linesides or linesider, squidhound, and zincsides

SCIENTIFIC NAME: *Morone saxatilis*

RANGE: Striped bass differ from many other marine species because, though they spend most of their lives in salt water, they run into fresh-water rivers along coasts to spawn or breed. They can adapt themselves to fresh water and, in fact, it has been discovered that they thrive in fresh water if there is enough food. As a result, stripers have been introduced into many inland rivers, lakes, and reservoirs in the United States. They have become a sport fish in both salt and fresh water.

Striped bass are found in the following areas:
1. Atlantic Coast—St. Lawrence River, Canada, to the St. Johns River in northern Florida
2. Gulf Coast—West coast of Florida to Louisiana
3. Pacific Coast—Columbia River, Washington, to central California
4. Inland waters such as the Santee-Cooper Reservoir, and Rio Grande and Colorado rivers.

PHYSICAL DESCRIPTION: The length of a striped bass is approximately four times its depth. Its longish head, mildly pointed snout, protruding lower jaw, and separated dorsal fins, combined with the seven or eight dark, greenish, narrow stripes running lengthwise along its body, make this species of bass easy to identify.

Coloring fluctuates but the dorsal surfaces are shades of greenish-olive to metallic-blue, with the sides greenish-silver turning to a whitish silvery hue on the belly.

Stripers range in weight from a few pounds on up to giants of 60 pounds or more, with the largest on record weighing 125 pounds. Female stripers of the same age as male stripers weigh more than the males.

Those states where stripers are present usually have laws governing the minimum length that may be kept by anglers. There also may be laws saying how many stripers an angler may keep from each day's catch. These regulations are to protect the species. It is important that you find out about them from the state's fish and game commission.

HABITS: Striped bass are voracious predators, feeding on smaller fishes, sea worms, eels, squid, mussels, soft shell clams, young lobsters, and other forms of sea life. The bass gorge themselves when they encounter schools of fish such as herring, mullet, menhaden, and other such species. At these times they may ignore an angler's baits and lures.

In their search for and pursuit of prey, stripers prowl at various levels, bottom to surface, and may be seen feeding on schools of small fishes that they have chased to the top. Since they are strong swimmers, they can also hunt food in a surf.

Often the best striped-bass fishing is from sunset until dawn when stripers are on the prowl for nocturnal creatures such as squid and eels.

FISHING PLACES: Coastal stripers prefer bays, inlets, deltas, estuaries, and the surf, while landlocked stripers appear to prefer deeper waters except in the spring and late summer months.

FISHING SEASONS: These vary according to the coasts because striped bass are migratory:

1. New England, New York, and New Jersey—best in spring and fall, with lesser catches during summer's hot weather
2. Maryland and Chesapeake Bay—best from March until December but caught all year
3. Virginia to St. Johns River in Florida—best in spring and autumn but caught all year
4. West coast of Florida to Louisiana—at this time there is no big fishery in the area but what stripers are caught are taken in the spring and summer
5. Columbia River, Washington, to central California— best fishing in late spring, summer, and fall but caught all year.

TACKLE: Both spinning and conventional types may be used, according to personal preference. Striped bass tackle ranges from light to medium, depending upon sizes of the fish currently running, angling methods, and personal ability of the fisherman involved—"personal ability" because it requires skill to handle husky, hard-fighting stripers on light gear. Tackle in the heavier class can be awkward and tiring for beginners to handle, yet may be required for the larger bass.

No one rod and reel outfit can be expected to handle all sizes of stripers satisfactorily for all methods and under all conditions. You should try different outfits to find out which best suits your kind of fishing.

HOOKS AND RIGGING: Hook sizes vary widely since they are

more or less gauged to the weights of the bass sought. This matching need not be precise, because stripers have big mouths. The important thing is that hooks be strong enough, No. 1 or 1/0 for "schoolies" (the smaller fish, so named because they travel in schools), up to 7/0 and 8/0 for the "lunkers" that can reach fifty pounds.

BAITS AND LURES: Striped bass respond to various kinds of natural bait and several types of artificials.

Natural baits include sandworm, bloodworm, clam, a strip of squid, whole small crab or piece of a large one, sand eels, whole American eels six to twelve inches long, chunks of fish such as menhaden, and strips cut from the lighter underside of other species.

Practically all the basic types of artificials have taken stripers at one time or another. These include spoons of various designs, plugs of all kinds, metal squids, and jigs of different types.

Since so many kinds of natural bait and artificials are involved, and since striped bass are unpredictable in their response, it is important to inquire locally—a tackle shop is a good place—to find out what the stripers are taking at that particular time.

FISHING METHODS: Striped bass may be caught by bottom fishing, trolling, shore casting, jigging, and by boat casting.

When rigging for trolling or jigging, whether using natural bait or an artificial, use a two-way swivel. Attach the end of your line to one end of the swivel and attach either the baited hook or artificial to the other end of the swivel.

For bottom fishing, boat casting, or shore casting use a three-way swivel or a fish-finder.

At whatever level you are fishing for stripers, only one hook of suitable size is rigged when using natural bait. Note that bank sinkers are used in rocky areas.

Whatever the method, keep your rigging simple. But since sometimes there are variations that are more effective in certain areas or at particular times, you should seek the suggestions of experienced local fishermen or tackle shops.

EDIBILITY: Excellent

Sea Bass

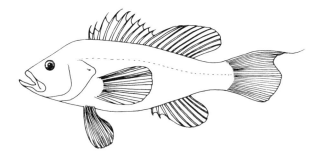

OTHER COMMON NAMES: Bass, black harry, black perch, black will, hannabill, rock bass, rock fish, talywag, and black sea bass

SCIENTIFIC NAME: *Centropristes striatus*

RANGE: Cape Cod to northern Florida. Regions of abundance extend from Long Island to North Carolina.

PHYSICAL DESCRIPTION: The sea bass is fairly stout bodied, with its length approximately three times more than its depth, the depth measured from the dorsal surface to the belly. These fish have a high, somewhat humped back with a flat-topped head tapering into a mildly pointed snout.

The fins of the sea bass are well developed and include a tail with an S-shaped edge. The long dorsal fin has a high, curved rear section. The forward portion of this fin has sharp spines, so anglers must use care in handling.

The coloring of the sea bass varies, but shades are mainly black, brown, gray, or blue-black, mixed with lighter-colored mottlings or bars on the back and sides. The belly is much lighter, almost whitish, in appearance.

Sea bass are fairly small, ranging from a few ounces to five pounds in weight. A world record specimen, however, weighed eight pounds. Smaller fish are known as "pin bass" while the heavier males with their high backs are called "humpbacks."

HABITS: Sea bass migrate into inshore waters during the early spring months where they remain until the chilly temperatures of autumn send them scurrying back to the deeper, warmer waters of the ocean.

FISHING PLACES: This species prefers clear water twenty to fifty feet deep over hard bottoms of rock or shellfish beds. Sea bass also frequent submerged wrecks, piers, and dock pilings where they feed on the crustaceans such as barnacles and mussels that grow on these structures.

FISHING SEASONS: In general the best season is from late spring to early fall. In more southerly parts of their range, some sea bass can be caught all year.

TACKLE: Light conventional or spinning gear will take most of the sea bass you are likely to encounter in coastal waters.

HOOKS AND RIGGING: Sea bass have large mouths, so hook sizes are not critical. A No. 1/0 or 2/0 will do for bay-running bass. For the larger, ocean-going fish, rig a 2/0 to 5/0.

Rig for the bottom, using either a Y-shaped rig or a high-low rig. On some fishing grounds, bass and porgies mingle (see Chapter 11, Porgies). With the high-low rig there is the chance of a mixed catch; the bottom hook is for sea bass while the top hook is for porgies. The top hook must be smaller than the bottom hook because of the porgy's smaller mouth.

Since sea bass are found primarily around submerged objects, there is always the chance, because of tides and current, of getting your rig snagged. Due to this fact, some anglers prefer fishing with just one hook tied by its snell right above the sinker. This reduces the possibility of snagging. Whatever rig is used, always attach a bank sinker to it. Because of snagging, carry spare hooks and sinkers.

BAITS AND LURES: Some sea bass are caught by trolling a small, shiny spoon very slowly along the sea or bay floor, but most of the fish are taken on natural baits, which, for ocean-running sea bass, include skimmer clam (ocean clam), hard-shell clam, or a piece of crab in the shedder state. (A shedder or "peeler" crab has cast off its shell so its body can grow. During this period its body is soft. After growth a new shell is formed.) These baits, along with bloodworm, sandworm, strips of squid, and pieces of fish, will attract bay-dwelling sea basses too. A bait of fair size can be put on the hook for these large-mouthed fish. Still another bait is a live killy, hooked through the lips and handled carefully so as not to injure it. An injured killy will not swim naturally.

One other artificial that is effective for sea bass is a diamond jig, so called because it is shaped like a long skinny diamond. Just tie it on your line and you are ready to fish. No bait is needed.

FISHING METHODS: The best method is bottom fishing at anchor with natural bait. Jigging can be especially effective around wrecks and reefs.

EDIBILITY: Excellent

Kelp Bass

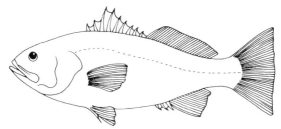

This fish, along with the spotted rock bass and the sand bass, belongs to a group called rock basses within the Serranidae family.

OTHER COMMON NAMES: Rock bass, calico bass, cabrilla, bull bass, and sand bass (also the name of another species)

SCIENTIFIC NAME: *Paralabrax clathratus*

RANGE: Central California southward to Cabo San Lucas, Baja California

PHYSICAL DESCRIPTION: Kelp basses have typical bass bodies, including a straight-edged tail. Dorsal surfaces are mottled with shades of dark brown or gray splotches over lighter hues of brownish-greenish gray. The lower sides and belly are colored in tones of silvery white, tinged with yellow.

A deeply cut notch between the first and second dorsal fins distinguishes kelp bass from sand and spotted rock basses.

Kelp basses average less than a pound though some occasionally attain weights up to five pounds.

HABITS: As its name denotes, this species prefers waters that harbor kelp beds and other sea grasses where crustaceans and smaller fishes shelter.

Studies conducted by the California Department of Fish and Game reveal that kelp bass are stay-at-home fish, seldom traveling any great distance. Because their populations are localized, undersized kelp bass should be returned to the water alive and unhurt. Check current California fishing regulations concerning minimum keeping size for kelp bass.

FISHING PLACES: Kelp bass are caught in and around kelp beds along shorelines, in the surf, and in bays and estuaries.

FISHING SEASONS: Some kelp bass are hooked all year but the best time is from May until October.

TACKLE: Your choice, spinning or conventional. If you wield light tackle you will have a lot of action. Kelp bass are good fighters. With light tackle, though, you must be prepared for a little work if your rig gets tangled in the kelp.

HOOKS AND RIGGING: A No. 1 will do the job. A common rig is a single hook on a nylon or monofilament leader about three or four feet long.

BAITS AND LURES: Most kelp bass are caught on natural baits. Best is a small live anchovy. Kelp bass will accept other small, live fishes too. When not "spoiled" by live offerings, they will take strips or pieces of mackerel, queenfish, squid, and anchovy, as well as shrimp and abalone "trimming."

Artificials such as small plugs and spoons also catch kelp bass. Yellow or bronze is the color for plugs; spoons should be shiny.

FISHING METHODS: Kelp bass feed at different levels, bottom to surface. Therefore, they may be caught by bottom fishing while at anchor or drifting; casting from a boat or the shoreline; or while trolling.

Get as close as possible to a kelp bed—when bottom fishing from a boat, anchor directly over a kelp bed; if drifting, drift over kelp beds; when casting either from a boat or the shore, cast toward a kelp bed; when trolling, troll as close as possible without tangling your line in the kelp beds.

EDIBILITY: Good

Spotted Rock Bass

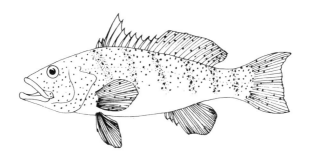

OTHER COMMON NAMES: Spotted bass, spotted sand bass, rock bass, spotted cabrilla, and pinta cabrilla

SCIENTIFIC NAME: *Paralabrax maculatofasciatus*

RANGE: Southern California to the Gulf of California

PHYSICAL DESCRIPTION: This species' dorsal surface, including the upper sides, is greenish or olive-brown in color, turning lighter on the lower sides until the coloring fades to a whitish hue on the belly. Six dim, dusky bands run vertically from the fish's back almost to the belly surface. Small, vividly prominent brown spots cover all areas except the belly, enabling the viewer to distinguish this species from the sand bass. Also, the lack of a deep notch between the first and second dorsal fins marks the difference between a spotted rock bass and a kelp bass.

HABITS: Spotted rock bass inhabit waters containing kelp beds or grass.

FISHING PLACES: Like the kelp and sand basses, this member of the rock bass group commonly inhabits close inshore waters and bays, often in the vicinity of rocky areas and sandy beaches. Spotted rock bass also are encountered in sloughs and lagoons adjacent to bays, as well as around the mouths of tributary streams.

FISHING SEASONS: Spotted rock bass are considered an all-year species.

TACKLE: Conventional or spinning, but light. Spotted rock bass are small fish. You will not need line any stronger than 6-pound test. Because of its flexibility, a light spinning rod is ideal.

HOOKS AND RIGGING: A No. 1 or slightly smaller No. 2 hook on a short, light leader will do. A three-way swivel will join line, leader, and bank sinker. The two- or three-foot leader can be attached anywhere from just above the sinker to a few inches above it.

BAITS AND LURES: Natural baits only are used. These include strips of fish, rock worm, clam, mussel, shrimp, and small live fishes.

FISHING METHODS: At anchor, on or near the bottom
EDIBILITY: Good

Sand Bass

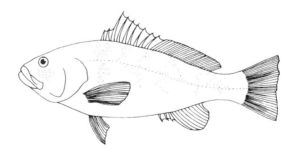

OTHER COMMON NAMES: California sand bass, Johnny Verde, and, mistakenly, kelp bass and rock bass
SCIENTIFIC NAME: *Paralabrax nebulifer*
RANGE: Central California to Baja California

PHYSICAL DESCRIPTION: Sand bass are customarily greenish-gray or greenish-brown with tinges of indistinct dusky, vertical stripes covering the sides of the body. The belly is white or pale grayish. Situated below the eye is an area that is usually covered with specks of gold and brown. Sand bass are distinguished from kelp bass by the absence of the deep notch between their first and second dorsal fins.

The average length for sand bass is eight inches, with large specimens to twenty inches. Sand bass average less than a pound, with some fish attaining weights of five pounds.

HABITS: Similar to those described for spotted rock bass. These fish also like sandy bottoms among rocks and near kelp beds. They are bottom feeders.

FISHING PLACES: In general, the same as for spotted bass

FISHING SEASONS: Sand bass, like the spotted rock bass, are considered an all-year species.

TACKLE: The same as for spotted rock bass

HOOKS AND RIGGING: Size No. 1 will do. Sand bass forage for food on the sea or bay floor, so rig accordingly. One or two hooks may be used, attached to the line either by their snells or by short, light leaders. You might try this arrangement: One hook just above the bank sinker for low-prowling bass, a second hook a half-foot to a foot or so above that for higher-cruising bass. This is another opportunity to experiment.

BAITS AND LURES: Natural baits, not artificials, catch these fish. Sand bass are not fussy eaters. They will take a strip of fish, a live anchovy or small sardine, and a shrimp or mussel.

FISHING METHODS: Fish the bottom at anchor near kelp beds and among weeds. Always carry spare hooks and sinkers when fishing these areas as rigs sometimes snag and cannot be pulled free.

If kelp beds and rocky areas are close to the shoreline, try shore casting. Use a light sinker or a sliding plastic float. Clip the float to the line so that it is free to slide up and down.

EDIBILITY: Good

 **8**

Bluefish: Among the Toughest Fighters

Bluefish are in a class by themselves in more ways than one. Not only are they the only known members of their family, Pomatomidae, but also, pound for pound, they are among the finest game fishes found anywhere in the world. Bluefish hit bait or lure savagely and are fast moving, powerful battlers that use all kinds of combat tactics. If some of the big game fishes, such as marlins, fought in the same proportion to their size as do bluefish, they could never be caught on today's rods and reels.

Bluefish have few equals when it comes to the attack. With mouths full of needle-sharp teeth, they go berserk when they taste the blood of prey. So savage are they that at times they practically drive fleeing prey up on shore.

Bluefish

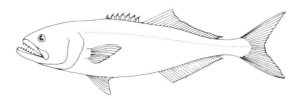

OTHER COMMON NAMES: Blue, chopper (because of their teeth and the way they use them), and tailor (possibly because their teeth can cut like a tailor's scissors)

There are also names for bluefish at various stages of their growth—when very young and weighing up to a pound or so, "snappers"; larger than that, to two and a half pounds, "snapper blues"; at three or four pounds, "harbor blues" (because at that size they often run into inlets, bays, and harbors); and from five pounds up they are known as bluefish. A world record 31¾-pound blue was caught at Hatteras Inlet, North Carolina.

SCIENTIFIC NAME: *Pomatomus saltatrix*

RANGE: Along the United States Atlantic Coast from southern New England to Florida and around into the Gulf of Mexico, where their distribution is not yet fully known. As far as is known, bluefish do not inhabit the Pacific Coast; yet they are encountered in such widely separated regions as the Mediterranean Sea and off the coasts of northern South America, South Africa, Malaya, Australia, and New Zealand.

PHYSICAL DESCRIPTION: The bluefish possesses a fairly long body, somewhat stocky in the middle but nicely streamlined. Other profile details include a sloping forehead, two dorsal fins (the second longer than the first), and a well-developed, deeply forked tail. The mouth is quite large, with a projecting lower jaw, and is armed with many strong, sharp teeth. Be extremely careful when handling bluefish. They bite!

Body colors, along the back and upper sides, are shades of blue, sometimes quite dark, sometimes greenish blue. The lower sides are shades of lighter hues of blue and green with the belly silvery. The fins are of the same general color as the upper parts of the body.

HABITS: Blues are oceanic fish roaming the seas in gigantic schools in their search for food. Always they are relentlessly on the move. As a result, an area may contain thousands of blues one day and none the next. Voracious predators, it almost seems that blues kill just for the love of butchery but undoubtedly this is nature's way of controlling the population of fishes in the sea.

When hunting bluefish, look for the surface disturbances they generate when feeding. The presence of sea gulls hovering over an area is an indicator that blues have chased their fleeing prey to the surface. Commonly blues feed at or near the surface but any level from there to the bottom has potential.

Although bluefish can be caught throughout daylight hours, the best times are early in the morning and late afternoon. They do not like midday heat, so at that time they go deep or move offshore to escape excessively warm water. During a storm, blues often move offshore or go deep where they remain a day or two. Some of the better bluefishing is at night, dusk to dawn, when blues seek nocturnal prey such as eels.

FISHING PLACES: Offshore and inshore in the ocean, in the surf, in and around inlets, in sounds, and in bays and harbors. Because bluefish schools are always on the prowl, it is usually a case of having to find them or being lucky enough to be in the right place at the right time.

FISHING SEASONS: Bluefish like temperate water. The best fishing months are from May through September, even into October. In more southerly sections of their range, such as North Carolina, some blues will linger deep into autumn, even into winter if waters are not too cold. Southern Florida has runs from late September through the winter into spring, and some blues are hooked all year.

TACKLE: Both conventional and spinning types are employed. Sizes of the blues currently running, methods, and anglers' ability determine the selection between light and medium tackle. Light gear will provide a lot of action with blues up to five or six pounds, but for larger choppers, beginners might better go to somewhat heavier tackle, using line up to 20-pound test.

For snappers—the "baby blues"—a popular outfit is a long cane pole. No reel is needed. A length of very light line is tied to the skinny tip. A single hook, No. 3 to No. 6, is baited with a killy or a spearing and dangled two or three feet below the surface with a plastic or cork float secured to the line. Snappers are as hard fighting as their elders, only smaller. Catching one on a bamboo pole is a lot of fun.

HOOKS AND RIGGING: Except for snappers, hook sizes go from about No. 1 or 1/0 up to 6/0 and 8/0 for the real heavyweights. Bluefish have roomy mouths and are eager to use them, so hook sizes are not critical. What is important is that hooks be sturdy and not rotted or corroded with rust. Since fishing for one bluefish at a time is usually enough action, only a single hook is rigged. Exceptions are artificials such as plugs and certain jigs that carry more than one hook.

Your basic bluefish rig—for all methods—consists merely of a leader and a hook or lure. The leader is connected to the line by a swivel. An ordinary two-loop barrel swivel is fine, and so is a small snap-swivel tied to the line, because it permits fast changing of rigs. Since bluefish schools move rapidly, feeding on a wide assortment of prey, a snap-swivel allowing quick changes between natural baits and artificials is the better choice.

Whatever your bluefishing method, you must have at least a foot or two of fine wire leader between your line and your hook or lure to guard against the choppers' sharp teeth. With snappers, a long-shank hook serves the same purpose.

BAITS AND LURES: It has been said that bluefish, when hungry, will snap at bubbles. In a feeding mood, they will respond to almost any kind of natural bait or artificial. Sometimes, though, it is necessary to experiment a little to see what they prefer.

Natural baits include strips or chunks cut from almost any kind of fish—menhaden (mossbunker), mackerel, mullet, even bluefish; small, whole butterfish or halves of larger ones; shrimp; strips of squid; small, whole eels; and chunks of crab.

As for lures, blues are caught on feathers, shiny spoons, cedar jigs, and other jigs with skirts of animal hairs or synthetic fibers, metal squid, and all kinds of plugs.

FISHING METHODS: Name any salt-water technique and it catches bluefish, but the most popular methods are trolling of artificials or strip baits and boat fishing with chum, either at anchor or drifting. Some of the largest catches are made by chumming with ground-up menhaden. Shore casting with plugs, metal squid, and natural eels also is popular.

Other methods are jigging (a diamond jig or similar artificial) at anchor or while drifting; casting natural baits and artificials from boats (when blues are surface feeding); deep trolling with wire line; and bottom fishing from boats and piers.

Blues are tricky battlers. One of their stunts is to change

direction suddenly when they "run," creating slack in the line. You must be prepared to reel in such slack immediately, otherwise your opponent may throw the hook free and escape.

EDIBILITY: Good. Many anglers prefer snappers, and the smaller blues to five pounds or so, for eating.

9

Croakers and Company: Finned Game for All

Some 150 different species of fishes, commonly called croakers, are included in the family Sciaenidae. Of this number, those fishes locally named weakfishes, drums, croakers, and whiting are most sought by anglers.

As the name croaker implies, the majority of these fishes have the unique ability to emit a croaking or drumming sound by vibrating their abdominal muscles against their air bladders. Croakers produce sounds in anger, fear, and hostility to rivals, as well as to attract mates during breeding. A few species are soundless due to their lack of an air bladder.

Croakers may be identified by a line that extends horizontally along their sides from their gills to the rim of the tail. Also, they have no more than two spines in the anal fin, and the front, rigid, spiny dorsal fin is near or at times attached to the rear, soft, rayed dorsal fin.

All species of Sciaenidae prefer warm water above a sandy bottom.

Weakfish

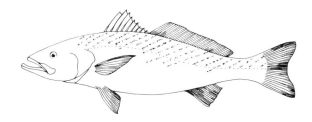

OTHER COMMON NAMES: Weak, gray weakfish, squeteague, yellowfin, tiderunner (the larger ones, in some areas), and, because of its troutlike form, gray trout, sea trout, and silver trout

SCIENTIFIC NAME: *Cynoscion regalis*

RANGE: Atlantic seaboard from Massachusetts to the tip of Florida

PHYSICAL DESCRIPTION: Weakfish are slim, streamlined, well-formed fish with colorings ranging from dark green to greenish-blue on their dorsal surface. Their sides are lightened with hues of gold, blue, green, purple, and lavender, giving these areas a coppery appearance. Both the dorsal surface and sides are covered with ill-defined small spots of black, dark green, or bronze. These spots flow together to form erratic lines which slant downward and forward.

The belly surface is white or silvery in color, often tinged with a yellowish-orange cast, while the tail is dusky-green with a yellowish lower rim. The dorsal fins are dusky and usually stained a yellowish hue, while the ventral, anal, and pectoral fins are always tinted yellow.

Weakfish have slightly pointed snouts, lower jaws that extend beyond the upper jaws, and large mouths. It is the mouth that earned the name of weakfish for this croaker. The angler must play the fish carefully so the hook does not tear through the soft-tissued mouth.

Weakfish range from half a pound to five pounds with some specimens weighing up to eleven or twelve pounds. Only the males of this species make a croaking noise and their thickened abdominal walls may be felt easily.

HABITS: Weakfish seek many types of food, traveling in large schools through fairly shallow water over sandy bottoms. They feed chiefly on smaller finned fishes such as butterfish, herring, menhaden, spearing, and killies. Weakfish also devour shrimps, crabs, and other crustaceans, as well as squid, marine worms, and mollusks.

Due to their varied diet, weaks frequent all levels of water, from the surface to the floor of the sea.

FISHING PLACES: Close-inshore ocean zones, including the surf, inlets, bays, sounds, channels, and quiet creeks, including those that wend their way through salt marshes

FISHING SEASONS: The best season is from late spring through September, but it can begin earlier and last longer in more southerly sections of the range. In northern sections the first two or three frosts usually "ring down the fishing curtain" in the fall. Often the largest weaks are hooked toward the end of the season.

TACKLE: A light, very flexible spinning or conventional rod will provide the most exciting sport with weaks, but demands care in playing the fish to avoid a popped line, possibly even a broken rod in the case of the largest weaks. Inexperienced fishermen had better use tackle handling at least 10-pound test line. Because it is designed primarily for casting, spinning tackle is superior for shorefishing.

HOOKS AND RIGGING: There is latitude in hook sizes because of the weakfish's rather large mouth. A 1/0 should handle just about all the weaks you will encounter.

BAITS AND LURES: Both natural food and man-made imitations are used. Baits include sandworm, shrimp, bloodworm, strips of squid, live killy, pieces of crab, and strips of flesh (porgy and others). Sometimes a combination of two kinds —like shrimp and a strip of squid, or a live killy and a squid strip—on the same hook is more effective than any one item alone. Artificials for weakfish include pearl squids, small shiny spoons, jigs, plastic worms and shrimp, and spinner rigs baited for added attraction.

FISHING METHODS: There are six favored methods—*top fishing, bottom fishing, jigging, trolling, shore casting*, and *casting from boats*.

1. *Top fishing:* A single hook is attached to the line through a nylon or monofilament leader two or three feet long. A two-loop barrel swivel between line and leader is optional. The boat can be anchored or allowed to drift. Establish a chum line by dropping small clusters of shrimp overboard. If currents tend to thrust the rig upward, it may be necessary to add tiny sinkers (split shot). Or, if there is little current, add a piece of cork to the rig to bring it up into the chum.

2. *Bottom fishing:* The best rig is the high-low rig. Bottom fishing for weaks can be done at anchor or while drifting slowly, the latter covering more territory. At anchor it helps to lift your high-low rig a few inches, let the current carry it a short distance, and then repeat the lifting process

again when it touches bottom. Don't let it get more than twenty feet from your boat or you will lose the feel of the fish hitting it. Try chumming with shrimp, ground-up fish, or cracked mussels.

3. *Jigging:* Since weakfish seek food at different levels, you never can be sure where they are. Jigging a small diamond rig, on a short leader, through various levels, bottom on up, can help to locate them. You can jig at anchor or while drifting.

4. *Trolling:* Not too many anglers troll for weaks because this method is not as productive as top fishing with chum, or bottom fishing. But it can account for some of the larger fish and provide great action because any fish responding to a trolled offering hits hard. In trolling, it may be necessary to experiment at different levels, near the surface and deeper, to locate weaks. A spinner rig baited with a whole sandworm is good and it might also hook a striped bass. Small shiny spoons also are trolled. Use a leader about three or four feet long, with or without a small barrel swivel.

5. *Shore casting:* For weakfish, shore casting is most likely to be productive when their run is well under way. A favored method is to work the bottom with a fish-finder rig baited with sandworm, bloodworm, or a piece of crab. Try a combination of worm and squid strip, too. Shore casting for weaks is great sport even though it does not catch as many fish as other methods. As it often requires considerable casting distance, use spinning tackle.

6. *Casting from boats:* This is a wide-open method because you can try different areas, baits, lures, depths, and speeds at which to crank your lines. Keep your bait or lure in motion by reeling in after each cast. Here, drifting is better than fishing at anchor because it covers more ground. If the drift or current is not too fast, try some chumming.

Important tips when fishing for weaks:

1. When boat fishing, be quiet. This species of Sciaenidae is noise-shy. If you anchor, ease the anchor into the water, do not drop it with a splash. Water carries sounds which weakfish can detect. Avoid heavy walking, dropping objects, and moving things around aboard the boat.

2. Play a weakfish carefully. If it wants to run (and it will), let it go. You can reel in later after the fish has lost some of its fight. And never "horse" a weakfish—that is, try to force it toward you—when playing it. Remember this fish's weak mouthparts. For the same reason, it is a good idea to have a landing net ready when lifting a weakfish from the water.

EDIBILITY: Good

Spotted Weakfish

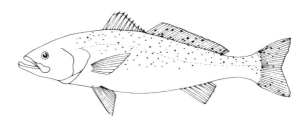

OTHER COMMON NAMES: Spotted sea trout, sea trout, spotted squeteague, spotted trout, southern weakfish, speckled trout (or speckles or specs), trout, and salmon trout—a thoroughly inappropriate name because this fish is neither a trout nor a salmon.

SCIENTIFIC NAME: *Cynoscion nebulosus*

RANGE: Chesapeake Bay to Florida, and the Gulf of Mexico to Texas

PHYSICAL DESCRIPTION: Spotted weakfish are shaped very much like their northern relative, *Cynoscion regalis*. Their dorsal surface is predominantly grayish, with lustrous shades of blue and purple that turn silvery on the sides. The belly is white. Unlike the more northern weakfish, the numerous round black spots (which account for the name) present on their upper sides extend onto the tail as well. All the fins are a light yellowish-green. On adults the dorsal fins and caudal fins are spotted in black.

In profile the spotted weakfish closely resembles its northern cousin, even to the size and shape of the head, large mouth, and projecting lower jaw. Color patterns help to separate the two species.

Mature fish average about four pounds, although seven- or eight-pound specimens are not uncommon. Some fish may weigh as much as twelve pounds but these are rare.

HABITS: Spotted weakfish spawn in shallow grassy beds in inland waters where they prefer to remain until cool weather sends them deeper.

FISHING PLACES: Best are shallow bays and their tributary coves and lagoons. Other areas with promise include the shallows over sand and mud flats and along the edges of shallow channels.

FISHING SEASONS: All year, but the best times are spring and fall.

TACKLE: The choice is the same as for northern weakfish, except that here you can stay on the light side. A good all-around combination is a light spinning rod, about six feet long, a small reel to match, and 6-pound test line.

HOOKS AND RIGGING: A No. 1 or 1/0 hook at the most. Rig as for top fishing with chum for northern weakfish.

BAITS AND LURES: Since spotted weakfish are so ravenous for shrimp, these small crustaceans are the best bait. But you can also attract weaks with strips or pieces of mullet, little crabs, and small, live baitfishes.

Successful artificials are plugs of various types—top-water and sinking models, jigs, and small bright spoons. Plugs with a silvery, flashy finish whose action imitates small fishes such as mullet are among the more effective lures.

FISHING METHODS: Spotted weakfish may be encountered at various levels, near-surface to near-bottom. Accordingly, methods include casting lures from boats and drift-fishing with natural bait, the baited hook at various intermediate levels in the water. Along the Gulf Coast, notably in Texas, many anglers like to wade the shallows while casting small artificials.

Popular along the Gulf Coast is a unique method called "splash poling." A long cane pole is used. To its outer tip is tied a length of light line that will extend a few feet below the surface of the water. To the line attach a bobber or float that can be adjusted to dangle a bait at a desired level. A single hook is rigged, on which is a live bait—shrimp, small mullet, pinfish, or some other local species. The method gets its odd name from the fact that at intervals the float and the tip of the cane pole are splashed at the surface to attract fish.

EDIBILITY: Good. The flesh of spotted weakfish spoils rapidly after capture. The fish should be cleaned and iced as soon as possible to prevent spoilage from taking place.

White Sea Bass

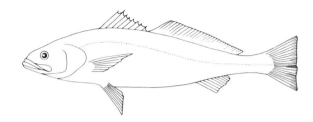

OTHER COMMON NAMES: California white sea bass, white croaker, king croaker, white sea trout, Catalina salmon, corbina, sand bass, and sea trout

SCIENTIFIC NAME: *Cynoscion nobilis*

RANGE: Alaska to South America, but mainly south from San Francisco

PHYSICAL DESCRIPTION: White sea bass are not bass but are members of the croaker family, closely resembling the weak-fish in configuration.

Top-side coloration shows tints of steel gray blending into a coppery, greenish-blue hue, with the sides turning silvery and the belly becoming a frosted pearly white.

White sea bass have large mouths, projecting lower jaws, and translucent dorsal fins that meet, with the first dorsal fin whitish-gray and the second a brownish-yellow. The tail is a transparent yellowish color. Pectoral fins are whitish, with the anal and ventral fins yellowish-white. There are no spots on any part of the body. Although ranging in size up to eighty pounds, specimens over forty pounds are rare, with the average about fifteen.

HABITS: White sea bass frequent warm waters near the

shoreline of islands where they spawn in kelp beds from early spring to mid-summer. Small fishes and squid make up most of their diet.

FISHING PLACES: Waters around kelp beds, in fairly shallow areas with sandy floors, along the edges of banks, and over shallow, submerged banks. The best areas are those in the vicinity of kelp beds.

FISHING SEASONS: White sea bass are caught all year in some areas, notably in more southerly sections of their range, but generally they are present in greater numbers from about May until September. Some of the best catches are made during the summer.

TACKLE: Since these fish reach a fair size, there is a chance of latching onto some fairly heavy ones, possibly up to twenty pounds or more. Unless you feel completely competent with spinning gear, conventional tackle is suggested—a rod able to handle lines up to 30-pound test.

HOOKS AND RIGGING: Hook sizes go from No. 1 to 2/0. Size is not a matter of precision, since sea bass have rather large mouths. The main thing is to have a hook strong enough for the heavier fish.

Since angling may be done in the vicinity of kelp beds, where there are always chances of a rig snagging, it is wise to use a simple, one-hook rig. Here is one version: The hook or lure goes on a three- or four-foot leader of nylon or monofilament (some anglers also use fine wire but this can be harder to handle). The leader can be about the same strength as the line or slightly heavier. Connect the leader to the line by a small, two-loop barrel swivel.

BAITS AND LURES: Highly recommended for the larger fish is a live squid. White sea bass will also seize large anchovies, medium-size sardines, very small mackerel, and strips of fish or squid. Most white sea bass are caught on natural baits but they also will respond to trolled artificials such as shiny spoons, plastic squid, and bone jigs.

FISHING METHODS: White sea bass feed at varying levels, commonly near the surface at night, near the bottom by day. Therefore they can be hooked by near-bottom fishing, trolling in the upper levels, or by letting a live bait drift out from the boat in shallow water. If a school of white sea bass is near the surface at night, you might try casting a bait or lure.

For bottom fishing you will need a sinker, bank for rocks or pyramid for sand. To attach sinker and leader, use a three-way swivel instead of the barrel swivel.

White sea bass, like weakfish, have weak mouthparts. You cannot force them. When they demand line in a run, let them take it and be prepared for a struggle. Play them carefully if they streak in among the kelp.

EDIBILITY: Good. The larger fish are best sliced into steaks; smaller ones are filleted.

Red Drum

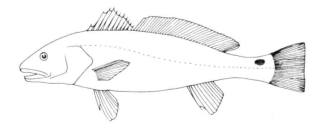

OTHER COMMON NAMES: Channel bass, redfish, bar bass, red horse, and spot tail. "Channel bass" is the most common name on the Atlantic Coast, but the bass is a misnomer.

Along the Gulf Coast you will seldom hear them referred to as anything but "redfish." The young fish are often called "puppy drums."

SCIENTIFIC NAME: *Sciaenops ocellata*

RANGE: Massachusetts to Florida, and into the Gulf of Mexico to Texas; however, they are seldom found north of New Jersey.

PHYSICAL DESCRIPTION: Red drum have short, slightly turned-up snouts, upper jaws that extend beyond their lower jaws, and bodies that are covered with broad scales. In almost every case, a conspicuously large, solid black spot is located at the point where the tail starts to fan out from the body. Some specimens may have two or three spots located on the base of the tail.

The dorsal surface of the species is colored in shades of olive-green to bluish-green, heightened with a copper- or bronze-toned hue. The sides are shimmering blends of gray, red, and pink which produce a coppery-bronze that lightens into pearly white on the belly.

Dorsal fins and tail are dark, anal and ventrals white, and pectorals ordinarily a radiant rust tone.

Sizes of red drum range down from forty pounds to the less than five pounds of the puppy drum. Average weight is about fifteen pounds.

HABITS: Red drum are bottom feeders, subsisting mainly on shrimp, crabs, and assorted small fishes.

In the Gulf of Mexico waters there is little evidence that the red drum migrate any great distance so they are at the mercy of the water temperature. This and other environmental conditions result in a fairly high rate of mortality, making the fish scarce at times. The situation does not appear to be a factor in Atlantic waters as red drum do migrate seasonally there.

FISHING PLACES: The surf beyond the breakers and in channels cutting through inlets, sounds, and bays. Many of the biggest drum have been taken from the Atlantic Coast surf, Virginia southward.

FISHING SEASONS: In Virginia, spring and autumn usually are best. In North Carolina the season is from March to November, and there can be surf-run fish into December. In Florida and along the Gulf Coast the season runs nearly through the year, with many redfish wintering in bays.

TACKLE: When shore casting for red drum, there are times when casting distance is required. Since spinning tackle is easier to use than conventional tackle, it is recommended. However, when casting distance is not required, use conventional tackle. If heavier drums are anticipated, lines go to 20- and 30-pound test. For most Gulf redfish, lines to 10-pound test are strong enough.

HOOKS AND RIGGING: Hook sizes are matched approximately to the general weight range of red drum in an area. They go from No. 1 or 1/0 for small fish up to No. 5/0 for big fish. Hooks should be strong. See Fishing Methods for rigging.

BAITS AND LURES: Live or dead shrimp, small live or dead crabs, strips of squid, pieces or strips of mullet. Artificials include jigs, spoons, metal squid, plugs of both surface (shallow water) and underwater types.

FISHING METHODS: From Virginia southward, shorefishing is popular, and it is the most exciting way to catch red drum. Rigs vary considerably and include a fish-finder for bottom fishing with bait and a leader when using lures.

In Virginia and North Carolina, red drum are also caught by trolling and casting from boats using natural baits and artificials. When casting artificials, reel in slowly as red drum often "play" with the lure before striking. Although not spectacular fighters, red drum are powerful fish that put up a determined, dogged fight. Bottom fishing, at anchor and drifting, accounts for a goodly number of these fish.

EDIBILITY: Opinions vary, according to taste. Generally the smaller red drums, up to twelve or fifteen pounds, are good eating. Fish larger than that have coarse meat and are only fair.

Black Drum

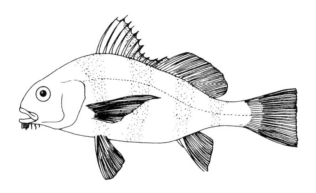

OTHER COMMON NAMES: Drum

SCIENTIFIC NAME: *Pogonias cromis*

RANGE: New Jersey to the northern waters of both the east and west coasts of Florida. Black drum are abundant off the coasts of Louisiana and Texas.

PHYSICAL DESCRIPTION: The snout of the black drum is blunt, and the mouth, housing large, flat teeth, is positioned horizontally and low on the face. The lower jaw has a number of short barbels (fleshy "whiskers") hanging from it.

Black drum have a hump-back silhouette. Their brassy-colored dorsal surface lightens into a silvery-gray hue on the sides and flattened belly. Young fish have four or five dusky bands covering their bodies that disappear as they mature. All fins are blackish in color with no spot present on the tail as in the red drum.

Black drums are one of the largest croaker species. Specimens in the twenty- to forty-pound class are quite common, and huskies up to sixty pounds have appeared in catches. The waters off Cape Charles, Virginia, have yielded two world-record fish, each weighing 111 pounds. At the other extreme are the numbers of black drum caught weighing less than ten pounds.

HABITS: Black drum like warm water and are primarily a coastal or inshore species. They travel in schools, feeding mainly on mollusks and crustaceans which they crush with their teeth. It is known, though, that they sometimes feed in the upper levels and near the surface when dense schools of such fishes as menhaden and pilchards are present. Black drums are noted for their ability to produce rather loud drumming or "purring" sounds.

FISHING PLACES: Black drums wander over sandy bottoms and shellfish beds close inshore, along beaches, and in the surf, as well as in inlet areas, sounds, bays, lagoons, and estuaries. Numbers of them are also found around bridges, docks, and piers where they feed upon the plentiful supply of mollusks and crustaceans there.

FISHING SEASONS: Spring into autumn. In Florida and sections of the Gulf Coast, black drums are considered an all-year species. Some areas see peak runs in spring and fall.

TACKLE: Although many black drum are small, their size potential should be kept in mind when choosing between spinning and conventional equipment. Also, the black drum's combat tactics are a factor. Although not a spectacular fighter, this fish puts up a stubborn resistance and stays deep, and one of good size has weight to add power to its fight. Black drums can be quite a contest in the surf, with currents and the fish's run adding to the action.

In shore casting, fairly heavy-duty spinning tackle is recommended. When bottom fishing, where casting is not essential, use conventional tackle capable of handling fairly heavy rigs. Twenty-pound test line is suggested.

HOOKS AND RIGGING: Because black drum have medium-size mouths, hook sizes do not have to be precise. It is more important that they be strong. Match them roughly to the weight of the drum expected, a 1/0 for the small fish and up to 5/0 and 6/0 for the larger ones. Rig for the bottom, one or two hooks. Leaders are not necessary. Tie your hook by its snell right above the sinker. If you rig a second one, tie that in by its snell a few inches above the first.

BAITS AND LURES: Black drum have been taken on various artificials but most are hooked with natural bait such as shrimp, whole shucked clam, a piece of mullet, or a small whole crab or a chunk of a larger one.

FISHING METHODS: Bottom fishing from boats, ocean piers, or jetties, and docks in inlets and channels. Many anglers prefer shorefishing, using a fish-finder or a simple, one-hook bottom rig, with a pyramid sinker for holding in sand.

EDIBILITY: Opinions differ, poor to fair. If any are eaten, they should be small, no larger than twelve pounds. The larger fish have coarse meat and poor flavor. By and large, black drums are more a sport fish than an eating fish.

Spot

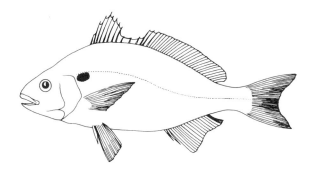

OTHER COMMON NAMES: Lafayette

SCIENTIFIC NAME: *Leiostomus xanthurus*

RANGE: The spot is commonly found from southern New Jersey southward along the Atlantic seaboard into the Gulf of Mexico as far as Texas.

PHYSICAL DESCRIPTION: Spots have short, stocky bodies and arched backs. Located above the pectoral fin and just behind the rim of the gill cover is the large black or yellowish-black spot which distinguishes this fish from all other croakers.

This species' dorsal and body surfaces are colored in shimmering shades of bluish-gray with metallic glazes of gold and bronze above, turning silvery on the lower sides and belly.

The twelve to fifteen diagonal, forward-slanting, yellowish bars that cover a young spot's body tend to fade as the fish matures. Also, the small teeth that immature spots have in their lower jaws are not present in adults. All specimens' fins are shadowy hues of yellow.

Size ranges up to fifteen inches, with the average fish

having less than two pounds of weight on its less than ten-inch body.

HABITS: Spots travel in schools in brackish and highly saline waters over sandy and muddy bottoms, feeding on small mollusks, little minnows, marine worms, small crustaceans, shrimp, and microscopic organisms known as plankton.

Generally spots stay rather close to shore, venturing into shallow areas, but they have been reported by commercial fishermen in depths of five hundred feet and more.

FISHING PLACES: The best areas for spot fishing are over oyster beds and in channels with eight or ten feet of water at high tides. At low tide, spots seek the deeper holes in channels.

FISHING SEASONS: Early spring into fall.

TACKLE: Light tackle is essential for spots, not only because of their size but also because they bite very gently. It requires a light, "sensitive" rod to feel their nibbles. Line, monofilament or braided, need be no stronger than 6-pound test.

HOOKS AND RIGGING: Rig for the bottom using quite small hooks—No. 10 to No. 8 will do. You may use from two to five hooks; usually at least three hooks are baited. No leaders are necessary: Tie your first hook into the line just above the sinker, and any others about three inches apart, with or without snells. Use the lightest possible sinker to keep your rig on the bottom.

BAITS AND LURES: No artificials, just natural baits. Spots will grab little shrimp and pieces of bloodworm, sandworm, crab, or fish. Baits must be in small pieces, just about enough to cover the hook's point and barb. Gently raise your rig off the bottom a couple of inches every few minutes. This will make the bait more attractive than if you let it lie quietly.

FISHING METHODS: Bottom fishing from oceanside piers and from boats in bays, sounds, estuaries, channels, and creeks

EDIBILITY: Fair. The meat is soft.

Yellowfin Croaker

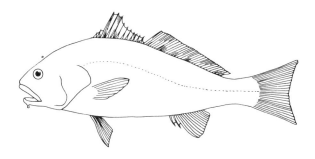

OTHER COMMON NAMES: Golden croaker, surf fish, yellow-finned recondor, and yellowtail

SCIENTIFIC NAME: *Umbrina roncador*

RANGE: Southern California to Baja California

PHYSICAL DESCRIPTION: An arched back, sloping forehead, and underside give this fish a deep-bodied appearance. There are two dorsal fins, typical in shape and size for members of this family, and they are connected, forming a deep notch. The tail has a slight V-indentation. The snout tapers to a rounded point that extends beyond the lower jaw, which has a small barbel suspended from the tip. This tiny barbel plus their sturdy anal spines easily distinguish this species from other West Coast croakers.

The color is a metallic green or gray, with brassy or golden reflections, becoming silvery below. Dark, wavy, greenish, or bluish lines extend downward and forward on the back and sides. The dorsal fins are dusky, the other fins yellowish.

Lengths go up to sixteen inches, maximum. Weights average in the neighborhood of one pound with some specimens weighing five pounds.

HABITS: Yellowfins prefer shallow water over sandy bottoms where they seek narrow channels near sandbars and banks. They are essentially bottom dwellers, feeding on small crustaceans, little fishes, and marine worms.

FISHING PLACES: This species is found in bays, inlets, and sometimes in the surf.

FISHING SEASONS: Yellowfins are caught all year but the best months are from late summer into autumn.

TACKLE: Size gives the clue—go as light as possible, spinning or conventional. These fish are good sport on very light tackle.

HOOKS AND RIGGING: Hooks are small, No. 1 or No. 2. Rig for near the bottom. A suggested rig is a two- or three-foot leader of very light monofilament, connected to the line via a three-way swivel about one foot above the sinker. Use only enough sinker weight to keep the rig on bottom.

BAITS AND LURES: Sandworms and pileworms are about the best baits. Mussels also work, as do shrimp, strips of anchovy, and sand crab in the soft-shell state. No artificials are used.

FISHING METHODS: Fish on or near the bottom.

EDIBILITY: Good

Atlantic Croaker

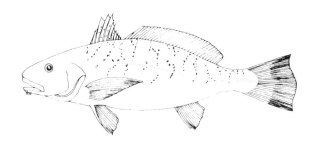

OTHER COMMON NAMES: Croaker, golden croaker, hard-head, grunt, grunter, corbina, crocus, and rocinda

SCIENTIFIC NAME: *Micropogon undulatus*

RANGE: Rhode Island to the Mid-Atlantic coastline of Florida. Also from Tampa Bay, Florida, across the Gulf of Mexico to Texas.

PHYSICAL DESCRIPTION: Atlantic croakers have an arched back, a lower jaw with barbels, and a mouth located low on its face with rows of small teeth in both jaws.

Dorsal surface and sides are colored with exceedingly light shades of gray, green, and silver. Irregular dusky bars slanting down the sides give the Atlantic croaker a metallic, dimly spotted appearance. Lower sides and belly are white. During spawning, the fish takes on a distinct yellowish hue, giving rise to the common name "golden croaker."

Average weight is about a pound, but three- or four-pound specimens are not uncommon.

HABITS: Atlantic croakers are schooling fish that like reasonably warm water. In common with their relatives, their movements are chiefly to offshore waters as colder weather approaches, then back inshore in the spring. The low position of the mouth on the head is a strong clue to bottom feeding habits. So are the barbels on the chin, which serve as sense organs to help locate food items. Diet consists of shrimp and other crustaceans, various kinds of small mollusks, and marine worms and other invertebrates. Favored areas include hard-packed sandy bottoms and those strewn with shells. Again like their relatives, these fish earn the name croaker by using certain muscles with the air bladder to produce sounds.

FISHING PLACES: Close-inshore ocean areas paralleling beaches, the surf, inlets, sounds, bays, and waters around coastal river mouths

FISHING SEASONS: Generally from April into October. In more southerly parts of their range they can arrive earlier and stay later.

TACKLE: Spinning or conventional, and it should be light, similar to that wielded for flounders and other species averaging under five pounds. A light spinning rod and line about 6-pound test are good. Atlantic croakers are lively scrappers on very light tackle.

HOOKS AND RIGGING: Keep your hooks on the small size with a No. 2 about the largest. Rig for the bottom. You can use one or two hooks. Leaders are not needed. Tie in your first hook by its snell, with or without a three-way swivel, immediately above the sinker. If you rig a second hook, tie that in similar fashion a few inches above the first.

BAITS AND LURES: Natural baits, no artificials. These fish will respond to shrimp, a piece of squid, bloodworm, and a piece of shedder crab.

FISHING METHODS: Bottom fishing exclusively. Aboard boat, either at anchor or while drifting slowly.

EDIBILITY: Good to excellent

Spotfin Croaker

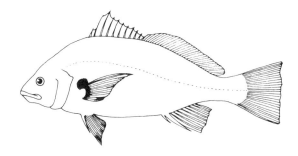

OTHER COMMON NAMES: Spot, surf fish, and golden croaker

SCIENTIFIC NAME: *Roncador stearnsi*

RANGE: Point Conception, California, southward and up into the Gulf of California

PHYSICAL DESCRIPTION: The snout of the fish is rounded and stretches beyond the lower jaw. The tail is squarish with the dorsal fins touching one another.

Body colorings are mixed metallic hues of blue, gray, and silver, giving the spotfin croaker a brassy, slightly golden sheen on the dorsal surface which blends into a silvery luster on the sides and belly.

A large black spot near the edge of the gills is located exactly at the point where the pectoral fins jut from the body.

Spotfin croakers weigh up to approximately twelve pounds with a maximum length of some thirty-six inches.

HABITS: Spotfin croakers live along ocean-front beaches and in bays, over bottoms varying from sand to mud, in depths that go as shallow as four or five feet to fifty feet or more. Usually they travel in small groups or in schools that number fewer than fifty individuals, although schools containing several hundred fish are encountered at times.

Spotfin croakers are bottom dwellers feeding on small crustaceans, mollusks, and sea worms that collect in depressions and holes at the sea's bottom.

FISHING PLACES: Surf beaches along sandy coasts, and in bays and sloughs. Anglers seek the so-called "croaker holes" in the surf and bays.

FISHING SEASONS: Some are caught all year, but the best months are from midsummer into autumn. Really good fishing seems to depend on spotfin runs. When these occur, angling is excellent.

TACKLE: Light spinning or conventional tackle with about 6-pound test line is fine.

HOOKS AND RIGGING: Hook sizes are small, No. 1 and No. 2. Rig for on or near the bottom, as for yellowfin croakers, but with short leaders.

BAITS AND LURES: Use only natural baits. Consistently good are sandworm, pileworm, mussel, and clam. Spotfins also take shrimp and sand crab, preferably in the soft-shell stage.

FISHING METHODS: Bottom angling in the surf and bays, and from piers

EDIBILITY: Excellent when breaded and fried

Northern King Whiting

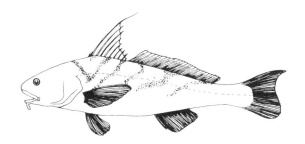

OTHER COMMON NAMES: Kingfish, king, northern kingfish, minkfish, whiting, and king whiting

SCIENTIFIC NAME: *Menticirrhus saxatilis*

RANGE: Cape Cod to Florida with the greatest concentration found from New York to Chesapeake Bay

PHYSICAL DESCRIPTION: Body colorings of northern king whiting are shimmering tones of dark lead-gray silver with the dorsal surface, at times, appearing almost black while the sides fade into a yellowish silver or creamy white hue on the belly. Darkish, irregular bars slant obliquely downward and forward from the back onto the sides with the first one or two of these slanting in the opposite direction to form a vague **V** above the pectoral fin. The fins are dusky or blackish except for the second dorsal which is tipped in white.

Northern king whiting have small mouths with bands of teeth in both jaws and a small barbel. These fish are unable to make drumming noises as they have no air bladder.

Average size for this species runs from half a pound up to a pound and a half with lengths from ten to fourteen inches.

HABITS: Northern king whiting are bottom feeders which travel in schools over hard, sandy bottoms, feeding mainly on crustaceans, sea worms, mollusks, and small fishes.

FISHING PLACES: During their seasonal visits to the coast they stay close to shore. Anglers find them in the ocean close inshore, in the surf, in and around inlets, and in bays, channels, and sounds.

FISHING SEASONS: The warm months, late spring through September, until waters begin to cool. Summer is best.

TACKLE: For kingfish the lightest kind, spinning or conventional. A light spinning outfit is good because of its casting "reach" in shorefishing; yet it can be used in a boat, too. Kings are scrappy fighters. If weakfish are in the same area, a common occurrence, it is wise to use heavier tackle as you might hook into a good-sized four- or five-pound weakfish.

HOOKS AND RIGGING: Kings do not have large mouths, so keep your hooks on the small size, no larger than No. 6 to No. 4.

BAITS AND LURES: Several baits are effective but should be in fairly small pieces—shrimp (whole when little), sandworm, bloodworm, squid, clam, a piece of shedder crab, and the so-called sand bug or sand flea found at the tide line along oceanfronts.

Northern king whiting usually do not respond well to artificials, but hits have been reported for very small spoons and worm-baited spinner rigs.

FISHING METHODS: All bottom angling.

1. *In the surf:* Use a fish-finder rig with a pyramid sinker to hold onto the bottom in rough surf waters. The hook can be on a short nylon or monofilament leader, two or three feet long, connected to your line by a barrel swivel.

2. *From a boat or pier:* Use a simple bottom rig connecting a three-way swivel to the line, a two- or three-foot leader, and a bank sinker having just enough weight to hold bottom.

The use of a bank sinker enables you to lift the rig off the bottom a few inches, letting the current carry it away from the boat a couple of hundred feet, then cranking it in without the sinker "biting" into the bottom as pyramid sinkers do. You need at least a couple of hundred yards of line for this.

EDIBILITY: Good

Southern King Whiting

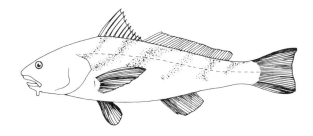

OTHER COMMON NAMES: Southern kingfish, king, and southern whiting

SCIENTIFIC NAME: *Menticirrhus americanus*

RANGE: New Jersey to Florida, then along the Gulf Coast to Texas, but in lesser numbers

PHYSICAL DESCRIPTION: This species of fish is similar to the northern king whiting in configuration, coloration, and size. However, the southern king whiting does not have any long, tapering dorsal spines nor any **V** formation above its pectoral fins.

HABITS: Southern king whiting are bottom feeders. They travel in schools over sandy bottoms feeding mainly on crustaceans, mollusks, sea worms, and small fishes.

FISHING PLACES: In general, about the same as for northern king whiting—bays, inlets, and swash channels (cuts through a sandbar) in the surf

FISHING SEASONS: Late spring into early fall with summer best

TACKLE: Very light spinning or conventional gear, the lighter the better

HOOKS AND RIGGING: Hooks should be fairly small, better undersized than too big. Nos. 6 to 4 should be about right.

BAITS AND LURES: Same as for northern king whiting

FISHING METHODS: Those suggested for northern king whiting, and the same rigging

EDIBILITY: Good

Gulf King Whiting

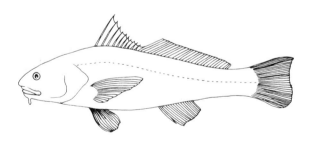

OTHER COMMON NAMES: Surf whiting

SCIENTIFIC NAME: *Menticirrhus littoralis*

RANGE: From Chesapeake Bay to and around Florida into the Gulf of Mexico to Texas

PHYSICAL DESCRIPTION: Although similar in configuration to the northern and southern king whiting, the gulf king whiting has a silvery-gray dorsal surface, bright silvery metallic sides, and a belly that is almost pure white. It lacks the dark-colored bands that extend over the other two species' bodies.

Average size ranges from half a pound to a pound with the maximum weight of two pounds.

HABITS: Gulf king whiting are bottom feeders. They seek out small crustaceans and mollusks on either hard or sandy surfaces.

FISHING PLACES: Shallow water in bays, inlets, and surf

FISHING SEASONS: The warmer months, spring through September

TACKLE: Very light, conventional or spinning, with spinning equipment favored

HOOKS AND RIGGING: Small hooks Nos. 6 to 4. And rig for the bottom.

BAITS AND LURES: Shrimp is the best bait, but pieces of fish, clam, and crab also get results. No artificials are used.

FISHING METHODS: Bottom angling, from a boat or a suitable shoreside location such as a dock or pier. You might try bridges also.

EDIBILITY: Good

California Corbina

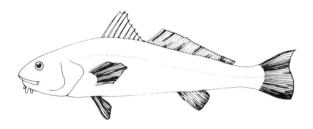

OTHER COMMON NAMES: California whiting, corbina or corvina, surf fish, and sea trout

SCIENTIFIC NAME: *Menticirrhus undulatus*

RANGE: Native to California where it is mainly found from Point Conception south to the Gulf of California

PHYSICAL DESCRIPTION: The body is relatively long and slender, characterized by a gracefully curving forehead and back with the belly flattish. The upper jaw extends beyond the lower jaw from which short meaty barbels hang. The dorsal surface is a shimmering bluish-gray metallic coloring which lightens into a grayish hue on the sides and becomes white on the belly. All of the corbina's fins are dusky in tone.

Maximum weight of corbinas is eight pounds with a length of eighteen to twenty inches.

HABITS: Corbinas are bottom-dwelling fish that feed on small crustaceans and mollusks that are caught in rough, swirling waters.

FISHING PLACES: This species frequents turbulent surf waters and bays over sandy bottoms.

FISHING SEASONS: All year, but angling generally is at its best from July through September.

TACKLE: Light, spinning or conventional. When casting in a surf, spinning gear may be better.

Hooks and rigging: Hooks are small, No. 2 or No. 1. Generally they are rigged for the bottom on a light four- or five-foot leader of nylon or monofilament.

The following rig can be used in any location: Tie a hook on a four- or five-foot leader and attach via a three-way swivel about one foot above a pyramid sinker.

Baits and lures: Natural baits only. Since sand crabs are the favorite food of the corbina they are excellent bait. Whenever possible they should be used in the soft-shell state. Other baits are bloodworm, pileworm, clam, mussel, and shrimp.

Fishing methods: Bottom angling in the surf, and in depressions in the bottom along sandy beaches and bays. High tide is an advantage in the surf because then corbinas come in closer and casts can be shorter.

Corbinas are very wary. Because of this and the way they feed—mouthing and chewing their food instead of hitting solidly—they can be difficult to hook, a good challenge. A suggestion is to reel the bait in very slowly, two or three feet at a time, with a pause before reeling again, instead of keeping it in constant motion.

Edibility: Excellent

10

Wrasses: "Throat-toothed" Fishes

Approximately 450 species of wrasses make up the family Labridae. All members of this family are noted for having pharyngeal or "throat teeth" which they use to crush their food—mainly barnacles and crustaceans. Although found mainly in tropical water, a few species live in temperate waters.

The majority of wrasses are quite small and not considered good sport fishes. But one species, the tautog, found in temperate waters off the northeastern coast of the United States, is not only a good sport fish but also a good food fish. The flesh, although tasty, is not extensively eaten because tautogs are difficult to clean in preparation for cooking.

Known as sea-going "bulldogs," tautogs are determined battlers.

Tautog

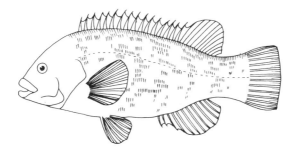

OTHER COMMON NAMES: Blackfish, black, oysterfish, moll, and whitechin

SCIENTIFIC NAME: *Tautoga onitis*

RANGE: Atlantic Coast of North America from Nova Scotia to South Carolina, but most abundant from New England to Delaware

PHYSICAL DESCRIPTION: A tautog's cloak of colors is anything but gaudy. This fish, in fact, is dark and rather drab. Its body color may be a dark gray mixed with black, a blend of chocolate brown and gray, a dusky black with a hint of dark green, or a dull black. When young, the sides are mottled or blotched with darker shades of the basic color. Larger tautogs turn almost plain black and have a conspicuous splash of white on the chin.

The color pattern is a camouflage, so shades and patterns vary according to those of the bottom on which the tautog happens to live. Generally the underside is only slightly paler than the rest of the body.

The most notable identifying details, in addition to the color pattern, are a chunky, solid-looking body and steeply

curving forehead; long, continuous dorsal fin, with a spiny
section and a soft, rounded rear portion; and a well-developed tail with a thick base. A physical detail of particular
importance to anglers is the mouth. It is low in the head and
is small with thick, tough lips, which means that hooks must
be small and needle sharp.

Tautogs commonly attain weights of eight to ten pounds
and may reach lengths up to two and a half feet. World
record weights go to twenty-one pounds.

HABITS: Tautogs are bottom feeders, eating mainly mussels, barnacles, and other such organisms that collect on
rocks, wrecks of ships, or submerged articles. They also devour shrimp, small crabs, clams, mussels, scallops, and young
lobsters. For this diet, tautogs are equipped with two sets of
teeth. In the front of the mouth are incisors for nipping of
barnacles and mussels; farther back are flat grinders for
crushing shells.

FISHING PLACES: Tautogs are strictly coastal residents,
never venturing far from shore into the ocean except to visit
offshore wrecks, reefs, and shellfish beds. This species frequent waters in rocky places, around jetties, pilings of docks
and piers, and submerged bases of bridges. Usually they are
in water no more than fifty or sixty feet deep. They also have
been known to feed among rocks and boulders in the surf.

FISHING SEASONS: Tautogs favor cool water, avoiding cold
and warm extremes. In winter they escape the cold in
deeper, warmer areas, remaining more or less inactive. With
the warming of spring they start to turn up on all their usual
grounds. There are two good seasons, in the spring from
early May until warmer weather; then again in the fall,
through October, when waters cool. Some can be caught in
deeper, cooler areas throughout the summer.

TACKLE: Tautogs are surprisingly strong fighters for their

size. When hooked they will run for any rocks or hiding places that may be handy, and the power surges of even a two-pounder are impressive. They live up to the nickname "bulldog." Conventional tackle is recommended over spinning tackle. It does not have to be heavy, but it should be able to handle lines to about 12-pound test.

HOOKS AND RIGGING: As noted, hooks must be kept fairly small because of the species' small mouth. Sizes No. 8 through No. 6 will handle bay tautogs. For larger tautogs, sizes increase to No. 3 and No. 2. The important thing is that the hooks be strong and very sharp.

Since tautogs feed on and near the bottom, rig accordingly. You can use one or two hooks. Tie your fishhook into the line by its snell right above the sinker, with or without a swivel. Your second hook is attached the same way, just far enough above the first so that they do not snarl each other. Another arrangement is the Y-shaped rig.

Because much tautog fishing is done among rocks and around wrecks and artificial reefs, there are good chances that your rig will become snagged sooner or later. You may be able to free it with your rod, or you may have to cut your line and rig all over again. In such places it often is better to rig only one hook to lessen chances of snagging. And always when fishing for tautogs carry spare hooks and sinkers. You will lose some of both.

BAITS AND LURES: Use natural baits exclusively, no artificials. Particularly good are fiddler crab and green crab. But tautogs also accept clam, bloodworm, sandworm, shrimp, pieces of periwinkle, and small baitfishes such as spearing and sand eels. A combination of shrimp and small pieces of clam also is effective. Sometimes during the early phases of their spring run, tautogs show a preference for soft baits, like worms or shucked clams, over hard baits such as crabs.

FISHING METHODS: Bottom angling from a boat at anchor, pier, dock, bridge, channel bank, or inlet jetty. At anchor you can chum with cracked mussels or clams, dropped overboard alongside the boat or in a meshed sack to bounce on the bottom.

Tautogs, with their tough mouths, can be tricky to hook because they tend to nip at a bait. Too, they may spit out a bait if they feel something suspicious. Be alert for nibbles, ready to set your hook with the rod tip when you think your tautog has the bait in its mouth.

EDIBILITY: Good. Tautogs are a little trouble to skin, but worth it.

Porgies: Popular Everywhere

Porgies, members of the Sparidae family, are small fish having flat, deeply compressed, saucer-shaped bodies. They are school fish that frequent Atlantic coastal waters in huge numbers during the warm months. Since many members of the family are tropical in distribution, uncommon, or too small, only two of the more popular species are presented here, the northern and southern porgies.

Porgies travel in schools. If you will move around the area that you are fishing, either in the ocean or bay, it will help you locate the schools and increase your chances of landing a good catch of porgies. If you don't hook some porgies at one spot in a reasonable length of time, move on to another location.

When the porgies are "in" there is little waiting time between catches. Not only are they fun to catch but they also make excellent eating.

Northern Porgy

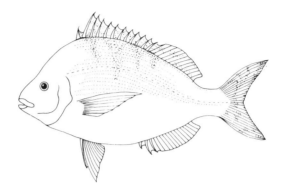

OTHER COMMON NAMES: Scup, porgy or pogey, and iron-sides

SCIENTIFIC NAME: Originally, *Stenotomus chrysops* but now *Stenotomus versicolor*, although both names are still used.

RANGE: From Maine to southern Florida

PHYSICAL DESCRIPTION: Northern porgies typically have deep-bodied configuration with short, snubbed snouts, small mouths, and slightly arched heads containing eyes set high on the head.

Body coloring of this species is a dark, glimmering, brownish-silvery tone on the dorsal surface, lightening on the sides to a whitish belly. Some fish may have several indistinct vertical bands, flecked with light blue, covering their sides. The fins are darkly mottled, except the pectorals which are transparent and the ventrals which are whitish.

Northern porgies average in weight from half a pound up

to two pounds with some specimens reaching a weight of four pounds.

HABITS: Northern porgies are bottom feeders that prefer warm water over clean, smooth, sandy bottoms.

FISHING PLACES: Ocean, bays, sounds, and channels. Young porgies venture into shallow bay waters in search of food, but the larger porgies remain in ocean waters no shallower than 6 to 12 feet or deeper than 90 to 120 feet.

Porgies and sea bass may be found on the same grounds in the summer. You can rig to catch both species. For details, see Hooks and Rigging under Sea Bass.

FISHING SEASONS: Late spring and summer months

TACKLE: Spinning or conventional, but light. The only times you might want it a bit heaver are in ocean fishing when fairly heavy sinkers are needed because of depths and currents, or perhaps when using a two-hook rig for porgies and another species.

HOOKS AND RIGGING: Keep your hooks small: No. 10 to No. 7 for the small bay porgies, No. 7 or No. 6 for the larger porgies. You can stay with one hook or use two, but rig for the bottom. No leaders are needed. Swivels are optional. Tie hook No. 1 by its snell right above the sinker, and No. 2 in a similar fashion just far enough above the first to prevent tangling. Or you can use a Y-shaped rig.

Sometimes weakfish and northern porgies are found together in bay waters. In this situation a high-low rig is recommended.

BAITS AND LURES: When they are in a feeding mood, porgies bite greedily. They accept a variety of baits that include shrimp, clam, bloodworm, sandworm, a piece of squid, a bit of crab, or a piece of fish. Use little pieces for the small bay fish. You can be more generous for the larger ocean porgies. No artificials are used.

Fishing methods: Exclusively bottom fishing, from boats chiefly, but also from piers, bridges, docks, and channel banks in suitable areas.

Edibility: Good. But do not try to scale them. They are among the toughest fish to scale. Skin them instead.

Southern Porgy

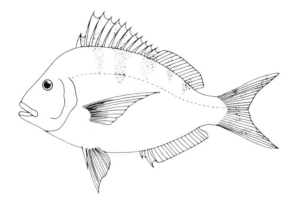

Other common names: Scup, porgy or pogey, and fair maid

Scientific name: *Stenotomus aculeatus*

Range: From around Cape Hatteras, North Carolina, southward to Florida, then into the Gulf of Mexico to Texas

Physical description: The southern porgy is similar to the northern porgy in almost all respects. Differences are quite fine and include, for the southern porgy, a less steep forehead and smaller size. Also, the southern porgy never has any longitudinal stripes covering its body.

HABITS: See Northern Porgy.

FISHING PLACES: See Northern Porgy.

FISHING SEASONS: Southern porgies are an all-year species in Florida and sections of their Gulf Coast distribution.

TACKLE: See Northern Porgy.

HOOKS AND RIGGING: See Northern Porgy.

BAITS AND LURES: See Northern Porgy.

FISHING METHODS: See Northern Porgy.

EDIBILITY: Like the northern porgy, good, but hard to scale. Skin them.

Index

SPECIAL LIST OF FISHES

Page reference to each fish covers: Baits and lures; Edibility; Fishing methods; Fishing places; Fishing seasons; Habits; Hooks and rigging; Names, common and scientific; Physical description; Range; Tackle.

Something about the authors

JOSEPH J. COOK, an Adjunct Associate Professor at Hofstra University on Long Island and a lifelong fisherman and observer of sea and shore life, is the author and co-author of a number of books for young readers. He has lived on Long Island all his life and gives many talks there to children and adults on the creatures that live in and near the sea.

WILLIAM L. WISNER is managing editor of the magazine *Long Island Sportsman*. A lifelong angler and student of the sea and its inhabitants, his articles have appeared in several national magazines and he has authored and co-authored a number of books about sport fishing and the sea. He resides on Long Island.

The authors have collaborated on *Coastal Fishing for Beginners*, *The Phantom World of the Octopus and Squid*, *The Nightmare World of the Shark*, *Killer Whale*, and *Blue Whale, Vanishing Leviathan*.